I0064664

Computational
by Design

First published in 2019
as part of the Design Principles and Practices Book Imprint
http://doi.org/10.18848/978-1-86335-123-2/CGP (Full Book)

BISAC Codes: DES007000, TEC016000, TEC009070

Common Ground Research Networks
2001 South First Street, Suite 202
University of Illinois Research Park
Champaign, IL
61820

Copyright © Viktor Malakuczi 2019

All rights reserved. Apart from fair dealing for the purposes of study, research, criticism or review as
   permitted under the applicable copyright legislation, no part of this book may be reproduced by any
   process without written permission from the publisher.

Library of Congress Cataloging-in-Publication Data

Names: Malakuczi, Viktor, author.
Title: Computational by design / Viktor Malakuczi.
Description: Champaign, IL : Common Ground Research Networks, [2019] | Includes bibliographical
   references and index.
Identifiers: LCCN 2018047158 (print) | LCCN 2018053187 (ebook) | ISBN 9781863351232 (pdf) |
   ISBN 9781863351218 (hardback : alk. paper) | ISBN 9781863351225 (pbk. : alk. paper)
Subjects: LCSH: Product design. | Computer-aided design. | Rapid prototyping. | Prototypes, Engineering.
Classification: LCC TS171.4 (ebook) | LCC TS171.4 .M354 2019 (print) | DDC 620/.00420285--dc23
LC record available at https://lccn.loc.gov/2018047158

Computational
by Design

Viktor Malakuczi

COMMON GROUND

DESIGN PRINCIPLES AND PRACTICES

Acknowledgements

This book is based on the research activities carried out at Sapienza University of Rome, over the three-year period of a doctorate in Planning, Design, Technologies of Architecture (30th cycle, PDTA Department).

First of all, I would like to sincerely thank my thesis supervisor Prof. Loredana Di Lucchio for the generous help and constructive criticism provided in all phases of the work, as well as for the opportunities offered for the experimentation. The research was backed by the collaboration of the Sapienza Design Factory laboratory and Marco Chialastri, who patiently supported prototyping with digital fabrication, in sometimes unconventional ways.

Workshops and didactic activities were essential for verifying the proposed design approach, so I am grateful for the precious feedback of all the students involved, as well as the contributions of Prof. Einar Stoltenberg from Oslo and fellow young researchers of Sapienza: Alex Coppola, Ainee Alamo Avila, Masha Zolotova. Furthermore, Gianni Denaro has kindly reviewed the entire text of the thesis work.

I fondly recall also the previous collaboration with the team of Makoo Jewels, which provided an impetus for researching computationally personalizable design.

Finally, I would like to thank Prof. Lorenzo Imbesi for the continuous support and motivation during the birth of this book.

Now consider what would happen
if the physical world outside computers was
as malleable as the digital world inside computers.
...
Personal fabrication will bring the programmability
of the digital worlds we've invented
to the physical world we inhabit.

Neil Gershenfeld, 2005

CONTENTS

PART I. **CONTEXT**

PART II. **PRACTICES**

PART III. **EVOLUTION**

INTRODUCTION

Recently Digital Fabrication equipment became widely accessible, as well as the tools of Computational Design (also called generative, parametric) which are ever more powerful and easier to use. Even though personalization has been long recognised as design principle that valorises the former two technologies, computationally personalizable and digitally fabricated products are still rare in the material culture. While technological limitations (to be overcome) play a role in this delay, this contribution argues that there is also a shortage of adequate conceptual capabilities on behalf of the Design profession.

Building on observations drawn from personalizable product case studies, the book develops a novel design approach, practicable through a canvas tool which helps to focus on user divergences, so that the adequate degrees of freedom can be left for a computational co-design process that (ideally) benefits from the creative contributions of the user. Hence, the title "Computational by Design" wants to suggest that computation in "Computational Design" shouldn't be used neither for the technology's sake, nor as an afterthought to please a few more people, nor for marginal improvements in physical performance, but it should be a new frontier of human-centered design based on a natively algorithmic thinking.

From mass production to computational co-design

"The variability of artifacts should match the diversity of their users. During the industrial era, designers believed that optimizing the efficiency of use by criteria they or other authorities had stipulated was universally desirable. Their products aimed at an enlightened majority of consumers, in the conviction that the remaining population could be taught or would comply, hardly realizing that this benefited mass production more so than individual users" (Krippendorff, 2006, p. 144). Of course, this fallacy of modernist thinking was soon recognised, leading to ever finer market segmentation and even mass customization. In the last three decades, this latter was adopted in some industries with varying success; experiences which highlighted that it's important to tackle not only with the manufacturing challenges, but also with establishing a well-calibrated solution space and an adequate choice navigation system.

Mass customization implied an intervention in mass manufacturing, but today as Digital Fabrication evolves, personalization can be taken to a far more ambitious level. More and more kinds of everyday objects can be effectively manufactured on demand with 3D printing, laser cutting and other rapid manufacturing tools, which question the need to produce these objects in invariable series. Digital platforms today involve an unprecedented amount of intellect in the production of media content, offering a worldwide stage to everyone. Can the same happen to the physical environment? For the foreseeable future, atoms will remain much harder to manipulate than bits, but in any case, it's easy to imagine a shift towards a more and more "malleable" material culture, so objects are becoming more and more a question of software. This future, however, would require a significant shift in the (product) designer's approach: as Maeda et al. (2017) argue, after the classical design focused on products, and after design thinking focused on organisations and systems, Computational Design renounces part of the control in favour of algorithms, trusting these to understand the individual requirements. Emerging from great quantities of data, Computational Design promises qualitatively different results, which can be both complex and fascinating, both seemingly simple but sophisticated in the background, thus improving the quality of life for many people.

This book focuses on promoting the diffusion of personalizable products in the material culture and in the near future; we are particularly interested in understanding the new skills and competences necessary for the transition from designing serial products to designing "natively" personalizable products. While technical knowledge regarding Digital Fabrication and Computational Design is already widely available, it is still challenging to identify commercially viable opportunities and to develop valid concepts. To do so, designers cannot pretend to fully understand the needs of all potential users and create just a few well-adjusted solutions – they need to design ways of gathering relevant user input and modifying the relevant attributes of the product, letting the user/co-designer to move within an adequately wide solution space. Of course, creating an unforeseeable multitude of products needs a different design approach compared to designing a single solution: user diversity should not be circumvented, but considered as a resource to create authentically personal artefacts.

A new thinking tool: Computational Concept Canvas

Albeit products with personalizable shape (through Parametric Design and Digital Manufacturing) are still rare in the material culture, much of the pioneering work has been already carried out: besides the many years of academic and industrial research, there are plenty of interesting commercialised products. A key insight came from these: to comprehend current strategies of personalization (thus promoting the diffusion of the practice), a series of case studies have been analyzed, which led to the understanding of several motivations why users could choose a personalizable product, nonetheless the usually higher price and slower acquisition compared to similar mass products. It was possible to identify 6 types of variabilities, dividable in two groups between mechanical and cognitive variabilities. Mechanical Variabilities imply personalization for physiology/ergonomics, environment/objects, function/performance reasons. Cognitive Variabilities imply personalization for aesthetic/emotional, social/cultural or narrative/experience reasons.

Based on these, the book suggests a design approach for the systematic replicating the observed personalization principles on any product typology, with the support of a new design tool: Computational Concept Canvas, which aims to guide the designer's thinking towards product concepts to which personalization is essential. The backbone of the work on the canvas is the examination of the chosen typology according to the six mentioned variabilities that could make personalization desirable. This analysis is completed with already existing frameworks and visual tools, such as the jobs-pains-gains analysis derived from the Value Proposition Canvas (Osterwalder et al., 2014), the widespread personas technique, the storyboarding of the customers journey, etc, all integrated in a large format canvas which stimulates the designer to consider a series of important factors and make it easy to follow the progress and identify roadblocks.

As a result, the designer can expect a concept that is mature enough for the onerous phase of computational modelling (e.g. Grasshopper, Processing, Three.js), with a confidence about the utility of personalization. So far, the canvas was tested mainly in a didactic setting; these experiences will be described in the last chapter.

The proposed tool might help designers to spread personalizable design across many product categories, thus creating new business opportunities coherently with the recent development of the Industry 4.0 paradigm. When used through online interfaces and automatized supply chains, Computational Design can act as a design partner which continuously re-shapes the product design, even in distant places or times – thus changing also the nature of participation in the design process. On the long term, this might promote a more active role of the user in shaping the material culture, enriching it with authentically personal artefacts according to the possibilities of the contemporary creative and productive environment, both through improving functionality and through new ways of creating meaning.

Book structure, chapter by chapter

The book is divided in three parts: Tendencies (chapter 1-2) Practices (chapter 3-4) and Evolution (chapter 5-8).

The first chapter collocates the book in the contemporary research and practice of Design, focusing on the shift from the passive consumer to the active prosumer, who can provide a creative contribution for product design. This raises novel innovation opportunities, but also hint at a shift in design methodology.

Chapter 2 explores ways of opening the design practice to contributions from the people, especially using digital technologies of collaboration and production. Practices such as mass customization, participatory design and open design are discussed, highlighting some virtuoso examples of harvesting collective intelligence, while interweaving real and virtual to create new experiences on the digital frontier.

Chapter 3 introduces Computational Design, which can effectively valorise the morphological freedom and logistical flexibility offered by Digital Fabrication, which is becoming an ever more realistic alternative to conventional technologies of serial production. The chapter overviews Computational Design history, purposes and technologies, distinguishing between three levels of abstraction, that determine also the difficulty of implementation, as well as the achievable diffusion and user experience.

Chapter 4 demonstrates best practices which productively use Computational Design and Digital Fabrication as means of creating products with flexible, user-modifiable form. A key observation is that user motivations for choosing a personalizable product can be classified among two main groups of factors: mechanical variabilities and cognitive variabilities, each of which is further divided in three categories.

Chapter 5 opens the third part of the book by arguing that the previously described tendencies and existing practices of personalizable design can be considered as a primordial state of a new design branch, which would build on subtle divergences among users, rather than generic needs. It is argued that such specialisation would require a specific concept design approach, in order to solidify the practice.

Chapter 6 proposes a new method for concept development, facilitated by the Computational Concept Canvas: a tool to help the conceptual development of meaningfully personalizable products. This chapter introduces the proposed workflow, the general principles and structure of the canvas, as well as the range of available formats.

Chapter 7 offers step by step instructions for compiling each of the 12 fields, organized in 3 modules.

Chapter 8 illustrates a series of didactic activities, both using the Computational Concept Canvas with the related workflow and using other approaches. The described situations range from a few days long workshop to an entire semester of teaching, all centred on personalizable design. Student projects demonstrate that the world of personalizable design can be extended according to all six kinds of variabilities identified in chapter 4.

Finally, the Conclusion reflects on the perspectives of human-centred, personalizable computational design the and the future development of the Design discipline.

PART I
CONTEXT
CHAPTER 1
A DESIGN SCENARIO

This chapter collocates the book in the contemporary research and practice of Design, which is becoming a generalisable discipline, applicable as much to processes, interfaces and information artefacts as to physical artefacts. We outline a scenario based on the recent technological and social evolution, which is transforming the entire chain of production-distribution-consumption in many product categories, changing also the perspectives of innovation, hence forecasting significant changes at least in some niches of Product Design. There is a shift towards a model of "on-demand design", which is going from a unidirectional condition to a bidirectional one: the passive consumer is becoming a proactive user, or prosumer, already widely involved in the production of digital content. Current technologies allow user involvement also in the definition of physical products, which does not necessarily derive from a static project to be replicated exactly, but they can be manufactured uniquely from a dynamic geometric model which integrates the (potentially creative) input of the end user. This shift requires a more open approach from Design professionals, who should focus on the idea of variability, based on divergences between users. Therefore, a methodological shift might be necessary, making this book a "Research for Design" contribution, to use the common distinction between design research approaches.

1.1 Design as discipline: definitions

This book reflects on a possible evolution of Design, so it is important to remember that the goals, activities and extent of this discipline are in continuous evolution, with often contrasting opinions. The roots of the Design profession and the conscious "design discourse" about industry and the material culture date back at least to the Arts&Crafts movement, continued by Deutscher Werkbund, Bauhaus, etc.; starting from the 1950s, Industrial Design have started to mature scientific communities in the major industrial countries, leading to a plurality of scientific-methodological approaches and a growing range of definitions. ICSID (International Council of Societies of Industrial Design) itself has adopted various definitions, such as this classical one of Maldonado (1969):

> *"Industrial design is a creative activity whose aims is to determine the formal qualities of objects produced by industry. These formal qualities are not only the external features but are principally those structural and functional relationships which convert a system to a coherent unity both from the point of view of the producer and the user. Industrial design extends to embrace all the aspects of human environment, which are conditioned by industrial production."*

More recently (2015), ICSID has updated both its naming to WDO (Word Design Organisation) and its definition of Design, making it even more inclusive and even trans-disciplinary:

> *"Industrial Design is a strategic problem-solving process that drives innovation, builds business success, and leads to a better quality of life through innovative products, systems, services, and experiences. Industrial Design bridges the gap between what is and what's possible. It is a trans-disciplinary profession that harnesses creativity to resolve problems and co-create solutions with the intent of making a product, system, service, experience or a business, better. At its heart, Industrial Design provides a more optimistic way of looking at the future by reframing problems as opportunities. It links innovation, technology, research, business, and customers to provide new value and competitive advantage across economic, social, and environmental spheres."*

A definition which, in its attempt to include all possible professional branches, limits itself to recognising a series of fields and principles of action on which designers can operate, rather than defining precisely their activities or role. This indicates an important shift: as Friedman notes already in 2008, design is becoming a generalisable discipline, ready to be applied as much to processes, interfaces and information artefacts as it is applicable to physical artefacts, fashion or advertisement. The multitude of fields obviously requires vastly divergent competences, even if the core principles of the human-centred approach remain the same.

1.2 Socio-economic scenario

The book's discourse on design can be collocated in the contemporary scenario by observing a series of recent phenomena related to the technological and social evolution which is transforming the entire chain of production-distribution-consumption in many product categories, changing also the perspectives of innovation:

- the maturing of Digital Fabrication technologies has led to its democratisation at every level of cost and quality, thus promoting its use as a tool for producing not only prototypes, but also durable consumer goods;
- the creative development of Maker communities releases a cognitive surplus generated by citizens who design together without disciplinary borders and produce useful things, without conventional company structure (Anderson, 2012);
- the shift towards *long tail economy* (Anderson, 2006) have increased the attention towards particular needs, especially thanks to the vastly more efficient global online commerce;
- the shift towards *experience economy* (Pine and Gilmore, 1999) favours the competitivity of products with a strong personal narrative;
- the renewed attention towards artisanal qualities (Micelli, 2011) indicates deep consumer interest in authenticity (Gilmore and Pine, 2007) and bespoke quality;
- the diffusion of industry 4.0 technologies, which is making mainstream product tailoring to individual customers (also known as *mass customization*, long practiced and matured by some industries).

Today, in the global market economy facilitated by online commerce, competitivity is strongly related to the capacity of product and process innovation; the recent democratisation of manufacturing technologies and technological knowledge seems particularly beneficial for small and medium enterprises (SMEs). It's safe to assume that the cited phenomena will bring significant changes at least in some niches of the Design discipline, which makes it timely to investigate novel product opportunities, as well as reviewing the creative process necessary for the optimal fruition of new manufacturing possibilities – reviewing in the same time also the necessary competences as well as the designer's role.

1.3 Digital fabrication as enabling technology

History in a nutshell

Among the mentioned phenomena, the firstly cited Digital Fabrication is central to our interest. The idea of directly transforming digital data in physical objects is not new at all: it originates at the dawn of computer history: MIT already in the 1950s started to experiment with CNC (computer numerical control) for subtractive production (machining). For decades, CAM (Computer Aided Manufacturing) systems were mainly used for precious special machinery, e.g. military or factory equipment, then the invention of additive manufacturing (3D printing) technologies in the 1980s led to the use of CNC machines as rapid prototyping tools, helping the design process at resourceful industrial actors. The slow evolution of these inventions (STL: stereolithography, SLS: selective laser sintering, FDM: fused deposit modelling, etc.) brought to the evolution of their application fields as well, from Rapid Prototyping to Rapid Manufacturing or even Desktop Manufacturing: some CNC machines are easy enough to use by non-experts, in environments that are traditionally considered places of "clean" intellectual work rather than "dirty" manufacturing. Such diffusion was sped up by many open source projects, stemming from the vision of self-replicating machines (RepRap project; Bowyer, 2007), which also stimulated an empowerment of the hidden creative capacities of citizens, through the reappropriation of the means of production which underpins the Maker movement (Anderson, 2012).

Regarding Digital Fabrication's impact on the world of manufacturing, there is a multitude of expectations; academics, entrepreneurs, educators or makers work for a multitude of objectives: powerful enterprises hope to serve better their clients and to stay in their leadership position, regional governments hope to boost local manufacturing and innovation and to increase jobs and taxes, while fab-labs and makerspaces promote the widespread diffusion of technological and manufacturing knowledge to benefit local communities, etc.

Expectations & reality

Popular press often suggests that the 3D printing revolution will substitute traditional manufacturing in a hardly specified "near future"; but what we can see so far is more of an incremental evolution of technologies invented in the 1980's. Compared to the also growing repertoire of serial production, these technologies still have numerous limitations, among which the reduced speed, an up to hundred times higher energy consumption compared to injection moulding (Yoon et al., 2014), higher material consumption, minor structural strength with a given geometry, minor – typically rough – surface quality, and limitations regarding food safety or electric components, not mentioning the typically higher price. Limitations are well-knowns even among vocal promoters of the 3D printing 'revolution': e.g. Gershenfeld (2012) foresees innovations like programmable matter, but he also admits that this will require further decades of evolution and significant investments. Beyond the advanced examples, 'cheap' 3D printers today also promote the countless reproductions of poorly designed, short-lived plastic objects with obviously negative environmental consequences as well as legal and ethical ambiguities (Lipson, 2013). There is also a vision of local fab-lab based production of digitally distributed designs, but as Holman (2016) points out, only a low percentage of users is ready to pay for Open Design, causing economic difficulties to the creators of such contents (i.e. designers).

Hence, the digitally fabricated consumer products are present in a relatively restricted range of the many product typologies, mainly decorative ones. Contrary to the expectations on the revolutionary potential of 3D printing, so far it turned out to be not very practical for fulfilling simple mechanical functionalities that are unvaried among large masses of people. There are many uses of 3D printing in niche B2B products, but for most consumer product categories it is not a reasonable choice: designers today must evaluate carefully if future users can gain more advantages from Digital Fabrication (logistical and morphological flexibility) or from conventional mass manufacturing (highly optimisable for quality and cost).

Despite current limitations, ever more often Digital Fabrication is a sustainable manufacturing option, so the relation between design and production changes, as the qualitative difference between prototyping and production disappears, and effective and efficient industrial production becomes available even to individual designers, artisans, makers or engineers. For them it is important to consider the limitations of Digital Fabrication, but also to benefit from its main competitive advantages as manufacturing technologies: the uniqueness of the results, as well as the potential morphological richness.

Industry 4.0

Digital Fabrication is part of a wider phenomenon, the long ongoing informatization in all industries, widely supported by governmental programs, often called with the popular term industry 4.0. This indicates a tendency in industrial automation which integrates new technologies to improve working conditions and to increase productivity and output quality. The term was coined in 2011 by a high-tech strategy of the German government, but it went widespread indicating the concept of smart factory, which involves the capillary diffusion of ICT systems for various goals, among which customization and logistical flexibility. Let's note that the term "industry 4.0" is often (and superficially) mixed up with the term "fourth industrial revolution", even though there is no consensus whether there is a qualitative revolution going on, or simply a quantitative development of technologies originated decades ago; indeed, there were various proclamations of the fourth industrial revolution in the past decades (Garbee, 2016). Anyways, World Economic Forum and its founder Klaus Schwab (2017) argue that there is actually a revolution going on, and Brynjolfsson e McAfee (2014) go even beyond, predicting a fundamentally different "second machine age", comparable in importance to the first industrial revolution, because it will allow even cognitive jobs to be automatized, thus substituting humans in many professions, unlike previous industrial revolutions which have simply amplified human capacities. In any case, thanks to the evolution (democratisation) of Digital Fabrication technologies and Internet of Things (IoT), the principles of Industry 4.0 are becoming applicable across many industries even with limited capital, like the small and micro enterprises, widespread across Europe.

Innovation implications

Digital Fabrication implies a new alignment between places and activities of design and production, as well as between virtual representation and physical manifestation of the ideas, naturally influencing the possibilities available to enterprises and designers. When production shifts from serial manufacturing (on costly custom-made equipment) to the direct conversion of digital data into physical objects (on standard machines), then:

- seriality isn't indispensable anymore for economically sustainable manufacturing (even though large batches remain easier to optimise)
- formal constraints become far less rigorous (but still existing)
- there new material possibilities (as well as new limitations)

These imply an important change in the design process: there is a more immediate relation between the designed geometry and the manufactured object, given the less need for production engineering optimisation, which could substantially change the product in the past. The immediateness brought by Digital Fabrication takes designers closer to the artisan's condition, who have a direct manual contact with their products. This kind of *renaissance* of the artisan's approach was already observed by McCullough (1996), who argued that the masterful manipulation of a design software can give a stimulating, material-like experience, similarly to the "analogue" artisan's experience. Moreover, if the designer materialises a digital model directly with desktop manufacturing, then a feedback loop is established, which allows a more sensible development according to the creative opportunities offered by the given design and production technology.

As far as the resulting product concerned, new technological opportunities imply new design opportunities as well, not only product, but also process innovations which change the relation between user and object. Regarding product innovations, Digital Fabrication allow novel mechanisms, material properties, as well as rich aesthetic languages which are significantly different from the previous ones, closer to the architectural style "parametricism" (e.g. Materialise MGX[1], Nervous systems[2], Co-de-iT[3]). Regarding process innovations, the decreasing importance of seriality leads to a substantial change in the chain of design-production-consumption. Consumption in the digital era assumes a more interactive nature, as Toffler (1980) foresaw decades ago, prosumers emerge: producers and consumers in the same time; a phenomenon manifested in the capillary diffusion of social media (YouTube, Facebook, Twitter) for immaterial artefacts, as well as in the Maker Movement for tangible objects.

Moreover, numerous examples of Design for Social Innovation highlight that today

---

[1] http://www.materialise.com/en/mgx/collection
[2] http://n-e-r-v-o-u-s.com/
[3] http://www.co-de-it.com

everyone can become a designer and improve their own living conditions (Manzini, 2015). The more proactive approach towards the consumption of information, environment and social conditions prefigures the (continued) "opening up" of the design and production of durable goods; therefore, we can assume a substantial change in the activities of Product Design.

> *"Using a metaphor from communication, the relation between Design, production and consumption shifts from a broadcasting condition, which is unidirectional (from one to many) of a specific content […] to an on-demand condition, which is above all interactive (from one to one) where content and competences are both flexible, as they conform to the needs of the interlocutor." (Di Lucchio, 2014, pp. 76-77, translated by V. M.)*

Another way to describe the difference is imagining the "modernist" approach to design, which focuses on the wellbeing of a large, generic group of clients, through the serial replica of the best possible solution to a well-defined problem. On the contrary, using Digital Fabrication, the production of every single product happens independently, making possible the production of diversified series on-demand, integrating also the creative contributions of users without a significant loss of efficiency, supposing an effective way for elaborating the necessary data. In order to valorise this potential of uniqueness, emerges the need to produce unique digital models, for which Computational (or parametric, generative) Design becomes particularly useful, as it enables the automatized production of an infinite variety of personalized geometries, as well as the development of "co-design" interfaces.

This raises the possibility to shift the attention of design from generic solutions to the specific needs of individuals. The book aims to offer a design approach for fully benefiting from the newly emerged opportunities, centred on the idea of variable design according to the specific user needs. To do so, we will explore not only technical, but also conceptual possibilities, considering that the recent CAD evolution enables generating complex variable geometries both offline and online, thus opening new frontiers of functional and morphological innovation in reach of a global audience.

1.4 A disciplinary problem

Recently we have seen many interesting technologies and examples developed for both Digital Fabrication and Computational (product) Design, beyond a significant scientific discourse both in design and in other disciplines (architecture, engineering, economic, etc.). Digital Fabrication was used for its capacity of facilitating the production of special equipment and precious tools for the manufacturing industry; later it became available for producing rapid prototypes, then for sophisticated unique pieces of art and design. However, its products haven't found yet a particularly relevant role in the everyday life; beyond the still limited performance, we can suspect that a reason for this lag is a shortage on behalf of the Design profession, which haven't found yet the right ways to valorise all the new creative opportunities, respecting the still relevant limits.

Computational Design seems to have an interesting potential for valorising the diffusion and democratisation of Digital Fabrication. So far, however, the noteworthy commercialised examples were concentrated in a few product categories, leaving uncertain the economic benefit of the professional specialisation necessary to the development of commercialisable projects with Computational Design. The limited variety of the application fields threatens the economic sustainability of the (product) designers specialising in this field, making it risky to embark on the onerous journey of learning Computational Design skills to a competitive level. In order to improve upon this situation, it would be desirable to extend consistently the actual range of product categories that employ Computational Design, towards today ignored product categories.

Therefore, beyond the technical competences, there might be a shortage of conceptual competences, hindering the identification of the right application fields and the development of competitive products that benefit from the characteristic advantages of the discussed technologies. Both of these tools are already used for product personalization or mass customization, to use a term connected to the previous era of mass production; in any case, personalization promises enterprises a competitive advantage on the saturated contemporary marketplace of advanced industrialised economies. Therefore, this book tackles with the scientific-disciplinary problem of increasing the knowledge and improving the practice of Design towards a more effective use of the new possibilities (Digital Fabrication and Computational Design), aiming at the best possible satisfaction of personal needs and desires, involving also the users' creative potential. We hypothesise that the development of personalizable objects could become a more consolidated practice with consistent results; this would require a concept design approach which is more aware of divergent needs. In particular, the book proposes a design methodology and design tool for the conceptual development focused on product variability according to the divergent user personalities.

Based on the outlined scientific problem, the book revolves around three main questions:

- How would it be possible to identify the product typologies of which personalization raises the perceived value enough to involve the user in the process?
- How would it be possible to develop a personalizable design that can adapt to the largest possible public?
- How would it be possible to offer users a more active and creative role in the definition of their artefacts?

1.5 Design methods

During the profession's history, Design had a strongly varying relation to hard sciences, from which it started to "import" a systemic approach in the 1960s, trying to solve the ever more numerous and complex problems of modern life. This attempt led to many proposals, but also to a disillusionment, as even some of the proponents of the first seminal Design Method conference of 1962, e.g. Cristopher Alexander e John Chris Jones, have subsequently renounced their previous efforts. One might argue that there is a recurring crisis of identity (self-perception) in the discipline: these are repeatedly resolved through new theories, fashions and ideologies, which eventually decrease designers' capacity to carry out everyday professional tasks, thus arriving to a new crisis, provoking the cyclical re-elaboration of theories and methods necessary for carrying out even the most basic design activities (Jonas, 2007). According to Cross (2007), "scientific" design methods face repeatedly this crisis because of a fundamental difference compared to hard sciences: *"There may indeed be a critical distinction to be made: method may be vital to the practice of science (where it validates the results) but not to the practice of design (where results do not have to be repeatable, and in most cases must not be repeated, or copied)"* (p. 43). He also observes that much of the industry-financed design research is manifested only in products rather than (scientific) publications, or even worse, much industrial research remains part of the companies' hidden wealth of knowledge. Friedman (2008) underlines the inevitable detachment between theory and practice: *"Moving from a general theory of design to the task of solving problems involves a significantly different mode of conceptualization and explicit knowledge management than adapting the tacit knowledge of individual design experience"* (p. 154). This is not to refuse the potential usefulness of scientific rigour, but to underline the need to choose the right method pragmatically – or, as this book will propose, to create it ad hoc for the kind of problem at hand. Arguing for the necessity of a methodological shift makes this volume a "Research for Design" contribution – in contrast with the "Research about Design" or "Research through Design" approaches, to use the common distinction between design research approaches (Stappers and Giaccardi, 2017).

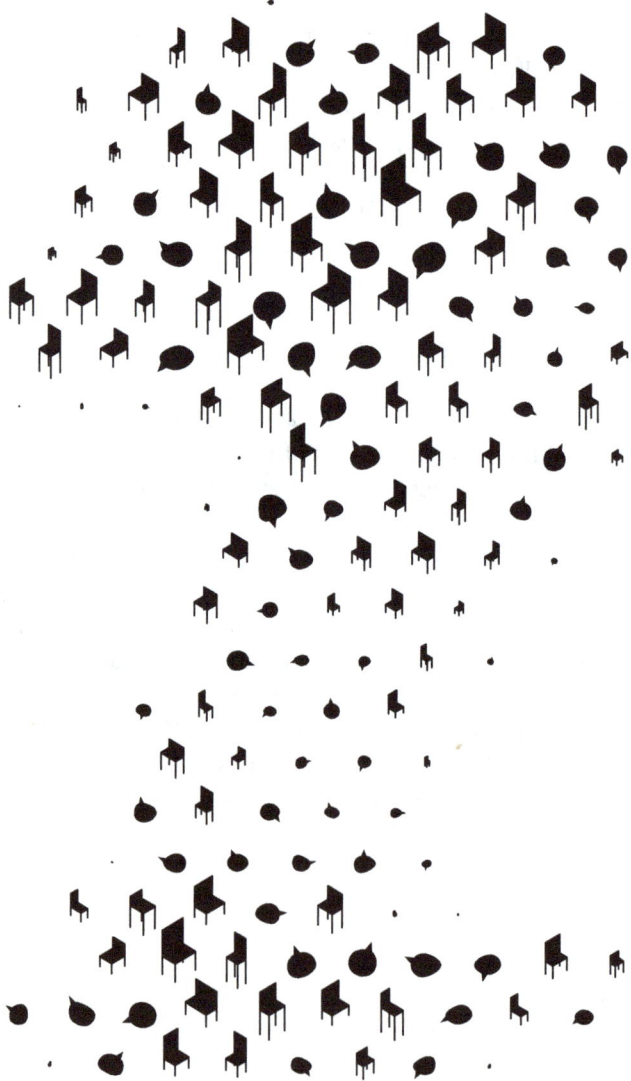

PART I
CONTEXT
CHAPTER 2
OPENING UP
PRODUCT DESIGN

This chapter explores ways of opening the design practice to contributions from the people, especially using digital technologies of collaboration and production. The idea of "personalization" existed already in the era of invariable mass production, as consumers were seeking products which could highlight their 'unique' personality. Then, as soon as the computerization of the assembly line made it possible to introduce combinations between components, the industrial practice of mass customization has emerged, allowing products in truly unique configurations instead of illusory uniqueness. This practice has generated a significant body of research both in industrial and academic context, underlining the importance of an adequate solution space and an effective way of navigating between the choices – requirements that go beyond the simple technological implementation of the diversified industrial production. The same principles can be considered as central to personalizable Computational Design. Parallel to the new industrial practices, also another, more profound way of user involvement has emerged: Participatory Design, already widely investigated by the scientific community, which have developed numerous ramifications and purposes. Using online platforms, Open Design can harvest the collective intelligence of creative professionals around the world, raising fundamentally new ways of product development. Moreover, the meta-designer can establish a multidimensional design space that allows also the user to become a co-designer. Continuous user feedback can even guide a progressive evolutionary development of designs, similarly to the mechanism of natural selection. Harvesting collective intelligence often relies on collaborations in a virtual space; real and virtual can be interwoven in order to create products and services that offer greater experiences by combining real and virtual elements.

2.1 The concept of personalization

The product now in demand is neither a staple nor a machine, it is a personality (Riesman, Denny and Glaze, 1950 p. 46)

Clearly 'personalization', far from being a mere advertising ploy, is actually a basic ideological concept of a society which 'personalizes' objects and beliefs solely in order to integrate persons more effectively. (Baudrillard, 1968, p.141)

This chapter explores some of the design approaches that recently have helped Design to satisfy the increasingly complex and particular user needs on the increasingly articulated contemporary market, but it is important to recognise that ever since competitive industrial production has emerged, it tried to personalize its offer. Already in 1968, Baudrillard argues that many (serial) products in "the system of objects" respond to a profound need for "personalization" in a certain sense: market segmentation happens through variations of the product typology's archetypical model, and these variations "personalize" the technical functionality of the product, donating a sensation of importance to the user – or consumer, to use the terminology of the era; consumerism of which he talks in a rather negative tone. Baudrillard saw a paradox in this personalization: at that time, it could mean only minor product differentiation adapting it to the main user groups – real, one to one industrial personalization wasn't yet practical. Therefore, people personalized their material culture by adhering to user groups (subcultures) which were already recognised, accepted and supported by the established industrial producers. The paradox was that by adapting design (style) to appeal consumer identities, industrial products tend to lose from their optimal technical performance – therefore, the system of industrial production "unscrupulously" plays with inessential elements to stimulate consumption. However, this might not to necessary anymore: ICT-infused factories widen the margins of effective and efficient personalization, and Digital Fabrication allows manufacturing unique objects (rather than exact copies) in a growing range of product categories.

As constraints of traditional seriality loosen up, it becomes possible to shift from illusory personalization (market segmentation, combinations, color, graphics) to a deeper, even morphological personalization of physical products. Digital Fabrication eliminates the need to produce numerous identical replicas to offer economically sustainable products. On the other hand, as Baudrillard notes,

it still cannot be denied that even superficial differences are real as soon as someone invests them with value. [...] No theory of needs can authorize us to assign priority to one actually experienced satisfaction over any other. If the demand for self-worth is so deep-seated that in the absence of any alternative it embodies itself in a 'personalized' object, what basis do we have for rejecting this tendency, and in the name of what 'authentic' essential value could we do so? (p. 153)

He concludes arguing that as long as the user considers an object a source of satisfaction, it is irrelevant that this was obtained by the marginal variation of inessential elements; the resulting satisfaction should be considered authentic anyways. In the contemporary design discipline, it is considered fundamental to curate the users' personal perceptions an all levels, including the totality of the related experiences, products and services. In particular, the perceived authenticity of experiences (with products or services) is a cultural construct, to be curated consciously, idea that Pine and Gilmore (1999 and 2007) discuss in their works revolving around "experience economy".

This book argues that, from a designer's perspective, Digital Fabrication and Computational Design should be promoted not only for the already well-explored possibility of producing particular shapes, or for the hoped shift to an alternative economic model, but also (and above all) for bringing closer production to every single user, respecting their divergent needs, desires and creative capabilities. In the context of contemporary economy, the suggested approach of 'deep' personalization can be seen as part of the *long tail economy* (Anderson, 2006), which foresaw the growth of the overall volume of niche products, thanks to distribution through online channels – far more effectively that it was possible though conventional 'brick and mortar' commerce.

The next chapters will explore ways of opening up product design towards users, while bringing closer the otherwise distinct steps of design, production, distribution and consumption.

2.2 Variability in serial production: mass customization

Anticipating the increasingly proactive role of the consumer in the post-industrial society, Toffler (1980) has foreseen the emerging figure of the 'prosumer' (producer+consumer) who contributes to the production of their artefacts, distinguishing themselves from the consumers of the industrial society, who were characterized by mass production, mass distribution, mass education, mass media and mass entertainment. As Krippendorff (2006, p. 144) expresses his critique of mass production,

> *"The variability of artifacts should match the diversity of their users. During the industrial era, designers believed that optimizing the efficiency of use by criteria they or other authorities had stipulated was universally desirable. Their products aimed at an enlightened majority of consumers, in the conviction that the remaining population could be taught or would comply, hardly realizing that this benefited mass production more so than individual users."*

Of course, this fallacy of modernist thinking was soon recognised, leading to ever finer market segmentation and eventually to *mass customization* thanks to the spreading informatisation of manufacturing facilities. Although Stan Davis coined the term already in 1987, *mass customization* was popularised by the seminal book of Pine (1992), who distinguished four categories of customization: (1) collaborative customization, where user input generates a substantial variation in the phase of production; (2) adaptive customization, where the product is modified directly by the user; (3) transparent customization, where the product is diversified without any perceivable moment of personalization; and, finally, (4) cosmetic customization which personalizes only the perception of a standard product, by presenting (or packaging) it differently.

The scope of personalization is strictly determined by the limited possibilities of intervention within mass manufacturing processes, if the producer wants to maintain efficiency, so Toffler's vision of *prosumers* is implemented to a very limited extent, usually. Initially, the main challenge was handing the interventions in the industrial process (engineering discipline) and conquering the trust of consumer (marketing discipline); in the meantime, form remained basically unvaried, focusing on graphical interventions or combinations between mass manufactured components. Still today, most examples of mass customization happens on the superficial level of colors and graphics; nonetheless, also these can reach a considerable success if they allow to distinguish that specific product among others: brands such as Nike or Adidas have demonstrated that even merely graphical variation can be sufficient to address a wide range of aesthetic tastes.

Naturally, Digital Fabrication allow progressively deeper personalization. As Davis (2007) puts it, "mass customization 2.0" has a bottom-up nature, similar to web 2.0 but acting on the material culture rather than media: consumers turn into a true *prosumers*, in the same time producers and consumers, who don't simply express preferences through to pre-established parameters, but also provide (creative) input which is indispensable for finalising the product.

In this context, the kind of intervention achievable by the user is a key element of success. The field has been widely explored by academic and industrial research, organized in communities such as the *Mass Customization Knowledge Network* or the *MIT Smart Customization Group;* starting from 2004, the biannual conference series *Mass Customization and Personalization Conferences (MCPC)* have gathered numerous experiences, described mainly with the perspective of business, management and engineering.

It's worth noting that, beyond the success stories, there have been high-level flops as well, such as Levi Strauss (which fell back to 'offering' do-it-yourself personalization). his shows that the profitable implementation of mass customization requires a particular constellation of conditions, starting from a concept well-fit to the identity of the brand.

To sum up their experiences in the sector, Salvador, Holan and Piller (2009) have identified a few recurring components of successful mass customization:

- •Solution Space Development: identify the attributes along which consumer needs diverge;
- •Robust Process Design: reuse and recombine existing resources to manufacture diversified products;
- •Choice Navigation: help the client to identify the best solution, reducing to the minimum the complexity and burden of choice.

These critical elements derive from the practice of differentiating serial products at manufacturing enterprises, but the observations seem equally useful also for the Design of personalizable products for Digital Fabrication and Computational Design. The growing family of Digital Fabrication tools (also at modest cost) is making more and more accessible the production of personalized series also at enterprises of small size and modest capitals; therefore, satisfying the second of the three cited criteria (Robust Process Design) is largely facilitated. It is still challenging, however, to come up with adequate Solution Spaces and intuitive ways of Choice Navigation; hence, these two merit additional attention and will be discussed further.

Solution Space

The most important difference between designing for mass production and for mass customization lies in the static nature of the first and the dynamic nature of the second. This difference means that it is necessary to expand the project from a single solution for a well-defined problem to a *solution space* which contains many possible projects. Mass production might serve the wellbeing of many users by replicating the product's advantages in countless copies; however, it copies also the eventual defects of the product, which can range from frustrating to disastrous, both for the user and for the enterprise. For this reason, the design profession has developed an obsession for perfection, and industrial designers' efforts are largely geared towards finding the best possible physical manifestation of a product concept, aiming at a single, 'perfect' project. Conversely, *mass customization* constrains the designer to renounce at least part of the control in favour of the final user. This might be seen as a way to lower the designer's responsibility: users have a way to express their preferences, therefore they 'must be happy' with the choice they make. However, it is still the designer's responsibility to offer a desirable base model with an adequate range of modifiable attributes which must be significant for the user – beyond, obviously, being technically feasible.

When potential user interventions are limited to colors or graphics, then the effort necessary to define the *solution space* is fairly limited: the project remains essentially unvaried, so successful *mass customization* is mostly an achievement of marketing, production engineering and logistics; designers' role is limited to hypothesizing some attractive variations. When the user configures a modular object made from mass produced components, then the designer must operate in a wider *solution space* to foresee typical (and atypical) configurations, understanding their aesthetic as well as functional and ergonomic implications. However, *solution spaces* acquire a real depth when personalization changes important dimensions, shapes and technical details of the product. In some cases, user input can lead to unforeseeable results, but the designer still needs to assume the responsibility of providing satisfying results, as well as providing only the truly necessary degrees of freedom.

Personalizing the geometry of a product is a far more risky and onerous operation compared to changing only colors and materials; therefore, even if Digital Fabrication is a reasonable option for realising the product, the designer must reflect deeply to understand whether eventual variations can really raise user satisfaction. Even if so, it's necessary to evaluate whether the provided advantages really justify the major effort of developing a reasonable *solution space* and the (likely) higher cost of the final product. For now, the still significant limitations of Digital Fabrication limit also personalization possibilities.

Regardless the width of the solution space, the organisation (or designer) must offer the user a well-calibrated interface, discussed below.

Choice Navigation

Helping the choice between different options might seem a task of marketing, but considering that the choices to navigate are defined in the solution space, we can see how strictly these two relate. Therefore, their integrated development is strongly advisable; the extent of the *solution space* and the 'interface' of *choice navigation* reciprocally determine each other.

In practice, most product configurators work on the web, which conveniently allows worldwide distribution without investing in retail infrastructure. Alternatively, an offline personalization process guided by expert personnel can be more reassuring for users who are less confident with digital technologies, especially if they see and touch physical product samples in the shop. Moreover, an offline personalization process can benefit from more advanced, professional CAD software, thus allowing more sophisticated geometries and a wider *solution space*. Finally, personal contact enables direct feedback, which can help to refine the *solution space* and optimise the parameters left open in the personalization interface; in this way, a physical shop can work as a laboratory for continuous experimentation, or as a pilot project for the subsequent development of an online configurator.

Regarding the possible interfaces of web-based personalization, there is already a significant body of experience: for example, the *Configurator Database Project*[1] has gathered more than a thousand configurators, focalised mostly on 'superficial' interventions regarding color, graphics or materials. On the other hand, there are still relatively few 3D configurators, in part because the live manipulation of 3D geometries is still relatively hard to implement, in part because the graphics quality

[1] https://www.configurator-database.com/database

is hard to guarantee due to the varying level of performance and software support on the users' widely varying devices. Nonetheless, evolving web technologies and platforms such as WebGL, ThreeJS, VerbNURBS, ShapeDiver, Twikit, Digital-Forming etc. promise to make it easier to implement 3D web configurators. Barriers are lowering also regarding automatized manufacturing: today various APIs (Application Programming Interfaces) can connect web configurators to online 3D printing service bureaus (i.Materialise, Shapeways), thus sending personalized geometries directly to these well-developed and maintained infrastructures for rapid outsourced production. These might seem merely technical considerations, but they imply that designers and companies can spare risky investments in machines, stock and logistics typical in mass manufacturing; such a light business model can allow designers to concentrate on the creative aspects of product development.

Discussing *choice navigation,* we should note that whenever an object is adapted to the body of the user (ergonomic personalization), such adaptation can happen in at least two ways: in simpler cases, a set of numeric parameters might be sufficient, which can be measured either by the producer or provided by the user. If a closer physiological adaptation is needed, it is possible through 3D scanning, not only with expensive professional equipment, but also with standard cameras (smartphone photogrammetry) or with depth cameras available in consumer electronics (Microsoft Kinect, Intel RealSense, Apple iPhone X).

When personalization revolves around cognitive aspects, most contemporary examples operate on a merely aesthetic level, offering some modifiable parameters and eventual textual or image input. The most engaging examples often contain a strong narrative element, connecting the product to certain characteristics of the user, or connecting the product to an interactive virtual world. In some cases, the computational personalization process results otherwise unobtainable geometries and concepts, fruit of a natively algorithmic thinking – most interesting from a Design perspective.

2.3 Participative Design, Co-Design, Open Design

Today the word "design" and "designer" are used in various ways. In English, it is used not only to identify the Industrial Design discipline and its derivatives/relatives, but the same word refers also to the 'creative' activity of architects, engineers and other professions, in particular it refers to imagining and describing something that doesn't exist yet.

The scope and tools of the Design discipline is widening continuously, as designers use a systemic approach to tackle with complex social, environmental, entrepreneurial problems. As Manzini (2015, p. 48) expresses, *"in our connected world, where everybody interacts with everyone else almost independently of time and distance, this separation of the design team from the rest of the world no longer stands. [...] So, in a connected world, all designing processes are in fact co-designing processes".*

The success of multi-, inter- or trans-disciplinary design practices such as IDEO has already demonstrated the potential of high-quality creative collaborations: experiences which they disseminate with various means, such as (in part free) design tools like *Design Kit: The Human-Centered Design Toolkit* or *Method cards*. IDEO CEO Tim Brown's influential book *Change by Design* (2009) helped to establish an important position for *design thinking* in the contemporary design discourse, arguing its importance not only for design professionals, but any organisation. As Bjögvinsson, Ehn and Hillgren (2012) notice, *design thinking* is, in a certain sense, a continuation of the socially sensitive Participatory Design tradition, which have emerged in the Scandinavian countries in the 1980's; however, *design thinking* has a more articulated and attractive rhetoric for the general public. This suggests that designers, rather than limiting themselves to products (things), should consider a wider picture of socially innovative design and open themselves to a collaborative effort together with all stakeholders, through an immediate approach of exploration and (rough) prototyping. Mostly in the European context, the principles of *design thinking* and *participatory design* have produced a significant quantity of research focused on *social innovation* – theorised and promoted by organisations such as the DESIS network (Design for Social Innovation and Sustainability) or the Young Foundation (Murray, Caulier-Grice and Mulgan, 2010).

So, the border between designer and user is melting in *social innovation* projects, and *participative design* increases mutual interaction in the research and concept phase of commercial projects as well. These phenomena can be connected to personalizable design as well: consumers have a growing voice in diversified production through a different way of participation: as discussed before, the established practice of *mass customization* involves the user in a (more or less creative) personalization process with an intuitive interface of *choice navigation* within a *solution space* (using the terminology of Salvador, de Holan, and Piller, 2009).

Finding an entire *solution space,* rather than a single solution, can be particularly challenging, as it requires designers to find product attributes on which consumers tend to *not* agree, i.e. they have divergent (rather than convergent) requirements. Leaving the possibility of some user intervention just before manufacturing eliminates the need to find the perfect consensus between contrasting opinions. Nonetheless, personalizability is not a substitute for user involvement in the early conceptual phase, which can raise surprising preferences and stimulate designers to amplify the borders of the solution space rather than shrinking them due to a limited understanding of the audience.

Anyways, after *open source software* and *open source hardware*, also *open design* is gaining traction, both in practice and research; De Mul (2011) emphasises the importance of the virtuoso handling of numerous variables, suggesting an interpretation of the designer's role as *meta-designer,* who designs a multidimensional solution space with a user-friendly interface, so that users become co-designers of their own artefacts. Based on the assumption that not all future uses and users can be foreseen, this approach creates open systems which can be modified directly by the users – in essence, *meta-design* is a design for designers (Fischer and Giaccardi, 2006).

Discussing complex IT systems, Fischer and Ostwald (2002) propose the *seeding, evolutionary growth, reseeding (SER) model:* an iterative approach based on the idea of starting with a small and simple project (seed) with ample potential of growth and change. According to this model, *meta-designers* start by constructing the 'seed project', which is incomplete or oversimplified, involving users in the system's evolution by asking many small contributions, i.e. feedback and suggestions. Then, the reseeding phase improves or even restructures the product/system, according to the suggestions gathered from the users.

Since Digital Fabrication minimises tooling costs, this *meta-design* approach of gradual evolution (comparable also to *lean development*) could become applicable also to physical products. However, as of today, online 3D modelling is still rather limited, so there aren't many noteworthy applications of the evolution-based development to physical products: a significative and unforeseeable evolution is extremely difficult to manage. One interesting example is the experimental platform Endlessforms.com, which allows the evolution of 3D geometries through an interface which takes user input as an evolutionary force to guide the development of virtual forms (Clune and Lipson, 2011). However, in absence of strong incentives to stimulate the contributions, there hasn't been a significant activity (or community) in recent years.

Relevant participation is achievable only when participants receive something valuable in exchange, reason why the precise calibration of this exchange must underpin every participative project which aims economically sustainable results (Brereton and Buur, 2008). DiSalvo et al. (2007) warn about the recurring illusion

Endlessforms.com web platform. The user guides the evolution of 3D shapes by choosing the desired direction of evolution among many similar geometries.
Center: a selection of 3D geometries, collaboratively generated on endlessforms.com
Bottom: some examples 3D printed with different technologies. Image source: www.shapeways.com/blog/archives/972-interview-with-jeff-clune-on-endlessforms-the-evolution-of-objects-for-3d-printing.html

of a motivated public out there, eagerly waiting and ready to participate actively to the project. On the contrary, they argue that such public must be constructed actively, organized and sustained through targeted actions and interventions of the designer or researcher. In order to provide a solid basis of participation, it should be clear what keeps together the people of a true community: for example, Armstrong and Hage (1999) classify the online communities according to four possible motivations: transaction, interest, fantasy or relations.

In any case, we can assert that the design discipline has an increasing capacity to involve users, considering them more and more the source of creative contributions, thus getting closer to the idea of the prosumer foreseen by Toffler. Further elaborating the concept of consumer culture as opposed to participative culture, Fischer (2009) notes the emergence of new in-between models with different levels of involvement, according to one's own experience or talent: beyond the prosumer, one can observe passionate experts, social production or mass collaboration. In order to guarantee the productive involvement of all these potentially useful actors, it is necessary to establish a highly structured collaboration. For example, Hess and Pipek (2012) have experimented with a delegation structure, organising participants in a so-called 'user parliament', overseen by a central committee composed of company representatives and prominent members of the user community, thus ensuring a voice for all stakeholders.

Another, even more structured – and even commercialised – example is Quirky: a platform that handles the development of products starting from so-called "inventions", selected by an online community; these ideas are further elaborated in collaboration with an internal team of designers, engineers, researchers and marketing experts. The precise tracking of the influencers is an extremely ambitious attempt to quantify contributions, and also a model of *crowdsourcing* that would be interesting to see spreading to other fields in the future.

However, there is a valid criticism towards *crowdsourcing* platforms: they tend to work simply as systems for gathering contributions, where people contribute with their own interests and abilities, while most of the crucial project activities (critics, analysis, improvements, extensions, negotiations...) do not happen here, as these are not particularly well-supported, so their value is not adequately recognised (Fischer, 2009). Such weakness of *open innovation* platforms is often imposed by the owner organisation itself which, more or less consciously, limit the dialogue between users when it establishes the collaboration channels (Singh and Gurumurthy, 2013). There is another important challenge for the application of collaborative software tools during new product development: a collaborative social ecology usually does not emerge automatically, but requires a conscious effort of stakeholder coordination, aiming to create the optimal conditions that guarantee productive participation (Yenicioglu and Suerdem, 2015).

2.4 Between real and virtual

Much of the "design opening" mentioned so far derives from the virtuoso use of digital technologies, that allow an unprecedented permeability between real and virtual. Using 'virtual' in the sense 'illusory', Maldonado already in 1992 notes that virtuality isn't particularly new: we humans always had the possibility (and impelling necessity) to delusively furnish the world. We have an obvious inclination to deceive ourselves, make the irreal real and vice versa. This happens through storytelling, by generating illusions, by believing (and making others believe) that these illusions are real. Without alarmism but in a troubled tone, Maldonado observes how the proliferation of the virtual could bring us to a culture of ephemeral; a forecast that seems rather accurate today.

The diffusion of virtuality brings new opportunities to Design, which can conceive experiences that move with agility between real and virtual, thus creating new, otherwise unobtainable values for the final user. Without denying that the most interesting experience will always (?) remain that what happens in the real world, Pine and Korn (2011) propose an interesting framework for comprehending and creating novel experiences on the digital frontier. They start form the observation that human experiences can be analyzed according to the 3 dimensions of the physical world: Space, Material and Time. In the virtuality, however, these three dimensions are inverted: the experience happens in a no-Space, with no-Matter in the no-Time – in a virtual space, with the matter of bits, in an autonomous time.

The key observation of Pine and Korn is that between the two extremes of complete reality and complete virtuality there are fine gradients distinguishable through the mentioned dimensions of Space, Matter and Time. Similarly to the semiotic square, which establishes four categories according to two opposing ends of two dimensions, the framework of Pine and Korn classifies experiences according to three dimensions, in a total of 2x2x2=8 "Realms", thus constructing a kind of 'semiotic cube' (term of free interpretation). The combinations of (real or virtual) Space, Matter and Time in each Realm imply qualitatively different experiences (near the initial of the dimensions, '+' or '-' indicate if that dimension is real or virtual in the given Realm):

- Reality (+S, +M, +T): defined by its sheer physicality, allows the richest experiences, involving all senses;
- Augmented Reality (+S, -M, +T): uses digital technologies (bits of the no-Matter) to increase the experience in the physical world, for example by explaining unknown aspects;
- Alternate Reality (+S, -M, -T): uses the physical world as a background for activities of virtual nature, connecting users to a fantasy world;
- Warped Reality (+S, +M, -T): manipulates time in some way to detach users from the everyday experience;

TIME
Times actual events:
the very realness of the now;
anticipation of waiting for events
that must occur in sequence; the
intensity ofthe course, rhythm, or
beat of real time; the satisfying
reward of mastering events in
actual time.
ACTUAL

NO-SPACE
No-Spaces virtual places:
the anticipation of fantasy and
imagination; the promise of
creatively conjured places; places
tailored to evoke emotions, offer
unique perspectives, hold out
new possibilities.
VIRTUAL

MATTER
Matters material
substances: the physicality of
matter, with all its roughness,
smoothness, heat, cold,
sharpness, dullness, shapes, and
so on; cool devices, tools, toys,
structures, and so forth.
ATOMS

NO-MATTER
No-Matters digital
substances: the accessing of
information; connecting; the
ability to express the creative
imagination; the anticipation of
newly expressed ideas, things,
and even worlds.
BITS

SPACE
Space's real places:
the perception of a real sense of
place; the promise ofrealness;
the familiarity ofthe physical
world around us.
REAL

NO-TIME
No-Times autonomus
events: the excitement of
experiencing another time;
the freedom of escaping the
now; the satisfaction of
insights gained from other
temporal perspectives; flow
experiences; escapes.
AUTONOMOUS

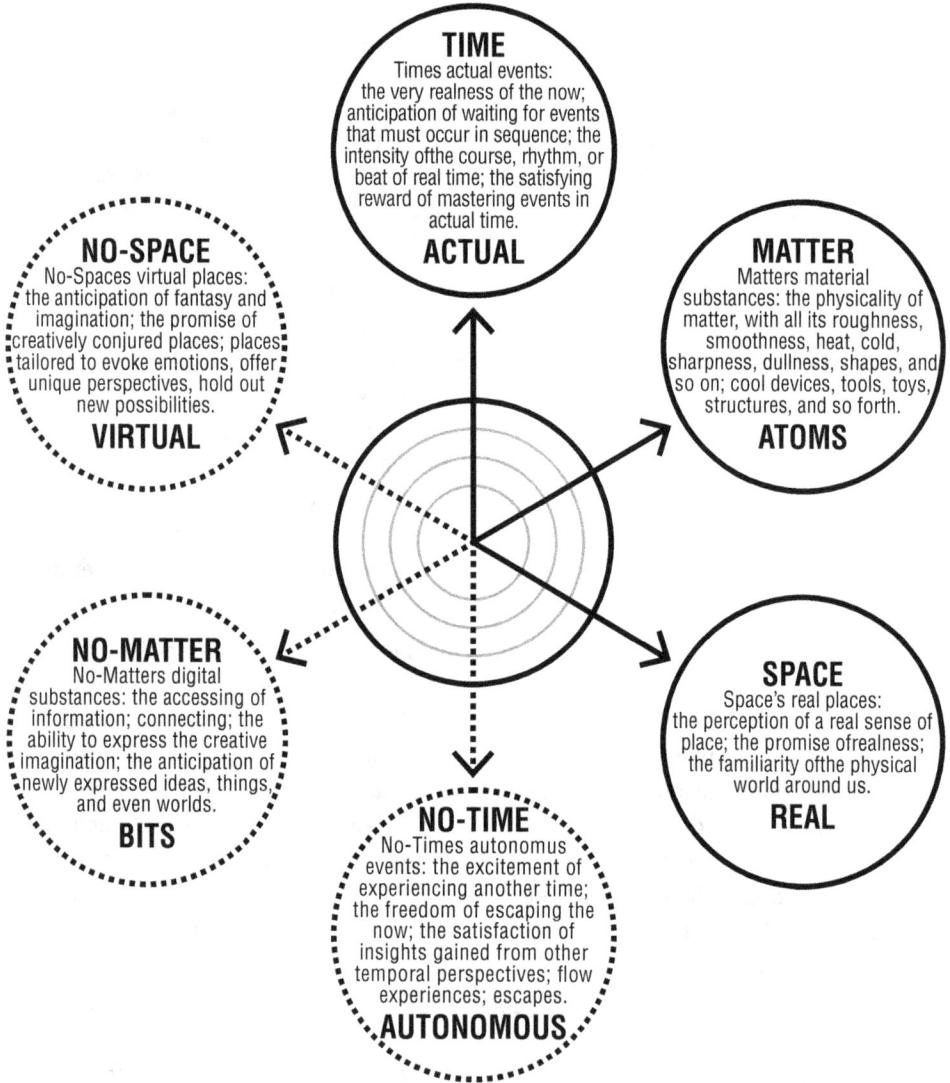

The axes and opposing dimensions of the "multiverse" framework proposed by Pine and Korn (2011).
The illustration is based on their book Infinite Possibility; the 'radar diagram' format is suggested by
these authors to facilitate the comprehension of the experience provided by any product or service.

AUGMENTED REALITY: Employ digital technology (the bits of No-Matter) to enhance our experience of the physical world, e.g. by making sense of it. WHO you are, WHERE you are, WHAT is around you, WHAT you are doing, and WHO is nearby.

Head Up Display (HUD), from military airplanes to normal cars
GPS navigation on any device   audioguides in museums
tourist apps: information overlaid on real world
Google glasses and Microsoft Hololens
Google Goggles visual search app
Layar Reality Browser application

TIME (ACTUAL)

MIRRORED VIRTUALITY: software models of some chunk of reality, some piece of the real world going on outside your window. Offers a real-time view, a mirrored perspective, of what is going on out there, in the world.
MLB Gameplay: follow sports, any angle
"Quantified self" devices & dashboards
Fitbit and other trackers
real-time flight tracker maps
HealthMap, Google Flu: map
disease spreading
Second Life

PHYSICAL VIRTUALITY: take real world objects (atoms residing in actual time) and designs them virtually: create, view, customize and sell online.
personalization apps on Shapeways, etc.
mass customization, from mugs to cars
custom production with 3D printing
LEGO Design byME (LEGO Digital
Designer): construct virtually,
get the necessary bricks
in a custom
pack

NO-SPACE (VIRTUAL)

MATTER (ATOMS)

PHYSICAL VIRTUALITY

VIRTUALITY: unfolding within the mind in reaction to the digital information (visual or audible). These experiences are not bound to a particular time or place, the physical aspects of the activity are irrelevant.
connecting via social media
surfing the World Wide Web
exploring virtual worlds
real-world simulations
computer games

MIRRORED VIRTUALITY

REALITY

AUGMENTED REALITY

VIRTUALITY

WARPED REALITY

ALTERNATE REALITY

REALITY: defined by its sheer physicality, Reality still presents the richest experiences of all the realms; its essence is to fully engage the five senses.
watching a sunset
going to a rock concert
dining with family or friends
skiing down a mountain
playing a round of golf
a walk in the woods

NO-MATTER (BITS)

AUGMENTED REALITY: making the physical world a technologically infused playground of hyperlinked activity.
GPS games like Geocaching
Interactive playgrounds and learning environments
Fantasy sports: real-life players, fantasy league
Google Ingress game   Pokemon Go
online Alternate Reality Games (ARGs)

WARPED REALITY: play with or manipulate time in some way that makes it clearly distinct and different from normal, workaday experience.
living history museums, e.g. Skansen
historical sport games, e.g. Florence football
historical reenactments, e.g. famous battles
renaissance & other fairs
Star Trek conventions

AUGMENTED VIRTUALITY

NO-TIME (AUTONOMOUS)

SPACE (REAL)

AUGMENTED VIRTUALITY: take something material and tactile and using it to augment an otherwise virtual experience. Similar to Augmented Reality, but the origin of the experience is different!
Nintendo's Wii & Balance board: on-screen games & movement
Videogame controllers: haptic feedback on shaking joystick
Playstation Move, Kinect gesture-based controllers
Guitar Hero, Dance Dance Revolution videogames
Cards for visualizing 3D contents with a webcam

Examples illustrating the "realms" in the "multiverse" framework of Pine and Korn (2011). The illustration is based on their book Infinite Possibility; the representation as a cube is suggested by these authors, as well as the examples cited around the cube. The graphics was elaborated by V. M., for use as a 'cheat sheet'.

- Virtuality (-S, -M, -T): creates an experience that reflects prevalently digital information, making therefore irrelevant all the physical circumstances of the user during the experience;
- Augmented Virtuality (-S, +M, -T): augments a prevalently virtual experience with something physical and tactile – might be confused with augmented reality, but here virtuality dominates the experience;
- Mirrored Virtuality (-S, -M, +T): recreates a relevant piece of the reality in the virtual space, but in real time, offering a different perspective;
- Physical Virtuality (-S, +M, +T): transforms something virtual in physical, using virtual interfaces to create real objects.

The last of these Realms highlight the relevance of the framework to the topic of the book: the promoted strategy of personalization through Computational Design for realising objects with Digital Fabrication clearly belongs to Physical Virtuality, where the user experience starts from the Virtuality, to become then Physical. Some of these experience Realms can be difficult to comprehend based on the previous, extremely synthetic explanation, so the included scheme illustrates each with examples, hopefully clarifying both the Realms' contents and their relation.

Anyways, this framework is a thinking tool which allows a more articulated comprehension of the perceivable user value of products and services which have a strong digital component. An interesting aspect from a Design perspective is that such a framework can stimulate the revitalisation of an existing product or service: after collocating it in one of the Realms (sub-cubes), the Design team can attempt to shift it to nearby ones by inverting gradually one or more of its dimensions. Such a gradual approach for evolving physical products towards virtuality (or vice versa) seems interesting not only in general, but also for a kind of conceptual connection to the technologies that this book aims to valorise: Digital Fabrication and Computational Design are technologies that bridge the gap between virtual (digital) information and the real world.

Having hinted how the experience with products (or services) can be forged between real and virtual, let's note that today more and more physical products have also a virtual identity, tracked through space and time thanks to the Internet of Things, turning products into what Sterling (2005) calls "spime" (space + time), objects which have their entire history automatically recorded. Sterling foresees a capillary diffusion of these 'intelligent' objects in the future, but already today we can observe the diffusion of this phenomena in industrial settings, which increasingly benefit from big data. On the other hand, also consumers are increasingly 'available' to be tracked when promised health benefits, which drive the *quantified self* movement. In a future where these objects become prevalent, there will be also abundant data flows which could potentially help to optimise products and to create authentically digital experiences and objects.

An intriguing frontier of personalizable design is the possible use of Artificial Intelligence for a deep computational understanding of user needs, which could lead to radically different ways of providing user input – this idea is taken to the extreme in the speculative design video "The Selfish Ledger" of Foster (2016, for Google X): a proactive register that gathers information about individual behaviour to construct a deep "understanding" about them and then to help them to achieve their long-term goals of personal growth. This AI could eventually generate automatically designs which are as useful and desirable as possible, based on previously owned objects and other data that could indicate a person's preferences – a clearly provocative idea, but could help to understand future possibilities on the long term.

Beyond technologist visions, the increasingly accurate knowledge of the surrounding world will allow to establish also increasingly sophisticated interaction through narratives that evolve with time. Chapman (2005) observes that most products have a very limited narrative capacity, almost exhausting it after few days or weeks of use, and the lack of a continuously maintained narrative leads to exhausting also the empathy of the user towards the object which, as a consequence, often gets discarded or substituted far before it becomes really unusable. Therefore, focusing on sustainability, Chapman urges designers to create and sustain strong and varied narratives to help creating emotionally durable products. This objective could be promoted by the increasing permeability between digital and physical, not only for smart products with integrated electronics and dynamic behaviours, but also for static products, which could be unique and unrepeatable if they benefitted from the digital opportunities in manufacturing and related services.

To conclude this chapter, let's return to Pine and Korn (2011) observing that at the end, what counts is the effectiveness of the experience, whether it is based on real or virtual stimulus:

> *"The experience happens inside each person. [...] the actual experience is your internal reaction to the external stimuli staged in front of you, whether those stimuli are generated via Reality, Virtuality, or a third space anywhere in between. All experiences truly exist only in the mind. [...] There's no escaping the reality: it's really all real [...] There's no escaping the verity: it's virtually all virtual. So design for the mind no matter what you want to do with the body."*
> *(e-book chapter 12)*

PART II
PRACTICES
CHAPTER 3
COMPUTATIONAL DESIGN FOR USER CO-DESIGN

While the previous chapter examined possible approaches to open up product design to user interventions, this chapter focuses more on the technologies this book aims to valorise. The strategic importance of Digital Fabrication is widely recognised, but its application in everyday life is still rather limited. Considering personalizable design a way to valorise Digital Fabrication, it is necessary to adopt a dynamic approach to 3D modelling, which is possible with tools of Computational Design, also called parametric or generative design/modelling. While the vision of dynamically configurable design inspired already the early CAD pioneers, the necessary software tools only recently matured to the point where even the Product Design discipline can implement and distribute them effectively (e.g. via web). Today, Computational Design is well known for its capacity to generate otherwise impossible complex geometries, which can lead to new aesthetic languages as well as a creative process enriched by algorithmic thinking at every stage, from idea generation to final detail optimisation. Designing with Computation is also comparable to the so-called workmanship of risk, which indicates the artisanal practice of working in strict collaboration with the material, letting the tools to guide the hand in order to obtain a result that benefits from the unforeseeable characteristics of the substance – which is a digital substance in this case. Anyways, since we are most interested in Computational Design's capacity to integrate user input into the design of every single product, we will also explore the possible tools and design approaches to do so, distinguishing design tools at three levels of abstraction.

3.1 "Computational" disambiguation

The term "Computational Design" can refer to various practices, and the way this book intends it differs significantly from typical motivations, such as generating complex geometries for optimised performance (engineering) or generating forms with an otherwise unobtainable morphological richness (the approach of many architects and artists). In fact, to distinguish between the many nuances of Computational Design, there are alternative terms such as parametric, algorithmic or generative design and modelling – and also the other way around, the term Computational Design is used also for designing purely digital artefacts (e.g. automatically personalized websites) or products with fixed shape but computationally enriched behaviours (smart objects, internet of things). The book focuses on physical objects, without venturing into the detailed discussion of the subtle differences between said branches of specialisation, as we are more interested in their diffusion across the material culture – therefore the most generic "Computational Design" term is used. Still, the next sections outline its origins, as this seems useful to understand its future evolution and the practical tools designers may use. The focus will remain on the potential of computational approaches to serve divergent human needs, raising the possibility to intervene significantly in the product's design before manufacturing with Digital Fabrication.

3.2 Digitalizing design: origins and vision

Digital Fabrication, as we have seen, eliminates part of the limitations imposed by seriality. On the other hand, benefitting from the new degrees of manufacturing freedom is possible only through an evolution in the way we generate the necessary input data, a step forward from the common 3D modelling tools used (and developed) to design static geometries for conventional manufacturing. In this software evolution, the architecture profession had a more important pioneering role compared to product design. In his *The Alphabet and the Algorithm*, Carpo (2015) discusses how digital technologies changed architecture on different levels, from education to practice and even legal conditions, but most importantly, Digital Fabrication and Computational Design helps to go beyond the fundamentally modernist approach of producing identical copies. In the history of architecture as a profession there were some key moments, such as the 15th century when the "architectural design project" was invented (Leon Battista Alberti), when the notion of the building as an exact copy of an architectural project was born. Then, starting in the 19th century, and especially in the modernity, building components became mass manufactured, just like industrial products and consumer goods. However, the dominance of identical copies could soon finish both in architecture and product design, thanks to Digital Fabrication, because whatever digital is easy to modify. Therefore, we can shift from a design creativity based on an alphabet of possible components towards an infinite inventory, derived fluidly from the specific requisites of the architectural project which is not codified anymore in static drawings, but in flexible algorithms.

From a technical perspective, transitioning from a static project to a dynamic project requires a very consciously structured parametric model, rather than the direct manipulation of surfaces, which is still a more popular approach in product design, albeit parametric solid modelling is also widely practiced (Llach, 2013). Parametric modelling allows changing the design in retrospect by changing some parameters of the already complete topological model – an idea born already in the pioneering era of CAD (1960's), when the development started from a belief in the transformative power of well-structured digital drawings. As CAD pioneer Sutherland argues, such transformation requires a profound change also in the way designers think: *"an ordinary draftsman is unconcerned with the structure of his drawing material. Pen and ink or pencil and paper have no inherent structure".* Instead, according to Sutherland (1975), the *"computerized version of the design [should be] the master document from which all auxiliary information is derived, preferably with computer assistance"* – this half century old idea is as useful for the new creative environment of makers, artisans and designers as it has been for the engineering community starting from the 1990's.

Ivan Sutherland demonstrates Sketchpad, an experimental software-hardware system of parametric CAD in the 1960's

3.3 Parametric modelling diffusion

Decades passed to get architectural practice close to the level of control imagined by Sutherland through the diffusion of BIM or Building Information Modelling. As far as (product) designers concerned, handling large quantities of construction data and extremely heavy geometries is less of a central concern, as the design process tend to involve in large part engineers of various specialisations (e.g. injection mould engineering), with their own software – so designer efforts revolve more about creating meaningful innovation and managing the collaboration with specialists who can handle technological-manufacturing complexity. However, products with personalizable shape require more of a 'total control' approach, which can foresee numerous outcomes, so "structured drawings" come useful to define solutions spaces.

The first functional prototype of a CAD program was Sketchpad by Sutherland, who coincidentally invented and developed the first ever graphical interface; already this 1963 software demonstrated many fundamental concepts of parametric modelling, such as the geometric constraints or dimensions that are modifiable

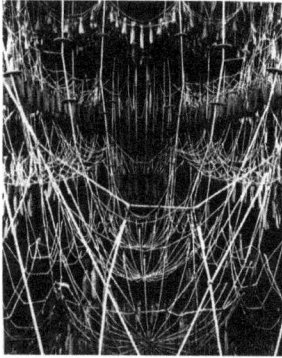

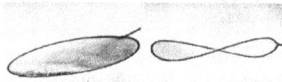

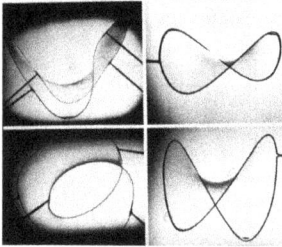

Parametric form finding to achieve the light architectural structures – by experimenting with analogue tools (Antoni Gaudí and Frei Otto)

in retrospect. These functionalities became available in engineering-focused CAD programs only starting from 1988. As PTC (Pro/Engineer) founder Geisberg expressed, with parametric modelling the goal is to create a system which is sufficiently flexible to encourage engineers to consider a wide variety of options in their projects, with a cost tending to zero in terms of time (as quoted in Davis, 2013). Parametric *solid modelling* tools were commercialised starting from the nineties, and soon adopted by engineers, for whom the deep integration between drawing, simulation and production is crucial – far more than for designers, who often prefer *freeform surface modelling*, which offers easier direct manipulation at the cost of physical fidelity. In architecture, the utilitarian parametric modelling paradigm called BIM (Building Information Modelling) was introduced in the 1980s with ArchiCAD; for a major morphological freedom, large architecture studios have developed their own solutions, such as the CATIA-based Digital Project at Frank Gehry's studio, used for his pioneering Guggenheim Museum at Bilbao in 1997, released in 2004 to the public; Davis (2013) gives a more comprehensive overview of the evolution of parametric modelling.

Starting from 2007, Grasshopper has democratised the design process of algorithmically generated geometries, thanks to its user-friendly interface which allows to manipulate mathematic operations in a visual way, controlling the flow of information between operations (nodes) through "wire" connections that are relatively easy to interpret also for people with a dominantly visual (artistic) sensibility, who could be alienated by textual programming languages. Tedeschi, Wirz and Andreani (2014) offer a detailed guide of how Grasshopper helps to practice an "algorithms-aided design", as they call this evolution of computer-aided design (CAD). The success of this tool is underpinned by the deep integration with the already familiar commands of a widespread CAD tool (Rhinoceros3D), which is not only capable and user-friendly, but also relatively affordable, hence popular among designers and architects. These latter also make use of a wide variety of Autodesk products, which are increasingly integrated with another visual programming language, Dynamo. Moreover, as we will discuss later, live parametric modelling is becoming available also through the web.

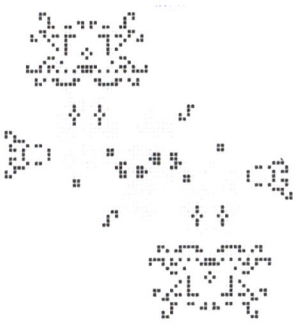

Mathematical experimentation with algorithms that generate complex patterns. On the left, an oscillating pattern from Conway's Game of Life. On the right, a Julia set, part of the more famous fractal Mandelbrot set.

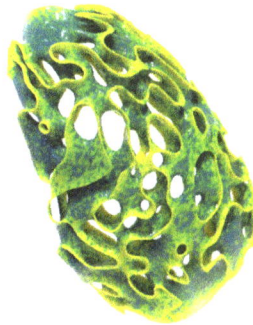

Evolution of the visual language: examples of the novel aesthetic qualities obtainable only through a 'natively' parametric design thinking – either in 2D or 3D
(John Maeda and Neri Oxman)

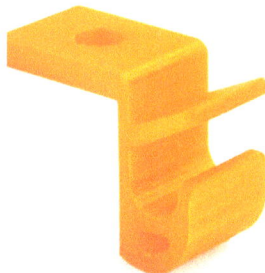

Using a parametric approach in product design, involving the user in processes of personalization with fundamentally different goals. On the left, the jewellery of Nervous Systems involves the user in a creative experience, leading to a decorative object.
On the right, the Parametric U-Hook of Serge Payen involves users to achieve functionality/performance perfectly corresponding to the specific requirements.

3.4 Computational visual language: evolving values

The current state of CAD evolution still hasn't completely fulfilled the vision of Sutherland, but in some sense, it went even beyond his original intent. First architecture, then design have started to use parametric modelling strategies beyond its original role as facilitator for realising preconceived ideas: they started to experiment with scripting languages as a medium that allows morphological research through algorithms.

> *[computer] is a medium that can dynamically simulate the details of any other medium, including media that cannot exist physically. It is not a tool, although it can act like many tools. It is the first metamedium, and as such it has degrees of freedom for representation and expression never before encountered. (Kay, 1984, p. 59)*

Actually, parametric form-finding was experimented already far before computers, see the analogous model based form-finding of Antoni Gaudí or Frei Otto, but these had the mostly quantitative scope of optimising already decided topologies. Digital algorithms, however, enable completely new morphological qualities. These often imitate natural growth, similarly to mathematical simulations of fractals (e.g. the Mandelbrot set, discovered/developed already in 1978), or logical 'organisms' governed by simple rules in a bidimensional matrix (Conway's Game of Life, 1970).

Starting from the 1990s, also architects and designers started to research and experiment with new and otherwise impossible geometries, popularising the approach with various publications, e.g. Greg Lynn (1993), John Maeda (2001), Neri Oxman (2010), Patrick Schumacher (2016). However, 'parametricism' as an architectural style remains controversial and often criticized for its (limited) practicality or efficiency, as well as its (presumed) disrespect for the pre-existing urban conditions. Analysing aesthetic adequacy is out of the scope of this book – we are trying to establish a more user-focused approach in Computational (Product) Design by allowing adaptation to user divergences, rather than promoting aesthetic values which are necessarily opinionable.

Anyways, regarding the appropriateness of "extreme" aesthetics, there is a noteworthy difference between architecture and design: architecture influences its environment for decades or even centuries and therefore should foresee and appeal to a wide range of users. On the other hand, privately owned products can adapt much more dynamically to individual aesthetic tastes, even to extreme ones – in fact, an important part of their job is to distinguish their owner from other people, as we have already discussed it through Baudrillard (1968); people are free to buy products without making a permanent mark on other people's environment.

Therefore, this book is mostly interested in Computational Design's potential to generate infinite morphological variations, derived from a continuous flow of user input which can establish a co-creation narrative, thus ensuring the emotional lon-gevity of the product. Hence, from a Product Design Perspective, the potential of new visual languages is only a part of why Computational Design seems promising: on the other hand, it allows to shift design authorship, sharing it with the end user. Such sharing of the creative act inevitably changes the design approach and the creative possibilities accessible to the designer. Design is a "humanist" profession which revolve around users and their values – and this book derives from the con-viction that when (product) designers use computational design tools, they should do so *first and foremost* to give space to all that the variety of human users could consider value – hence the title of the book is Computational *by* Design.

3.5 Computational creativity

The implications of Computational Design on visual languages might seem a ques-tion of ephemeral styles which change continuously, but the impact on the design process can be deeper, even though it is far more difficult to initiate this change. Renouncing total control and leaving open variables for actors beyond the designer itself (whether to data flows or end users) requires not only learning new (textual or visual) scripting tools, but also a change in the creative attitude.

Algorithm-aided creativity has been an area of research mostly in architecture, where the prolonged experience has produced many more in-depth inquiries com-pared to Product Design. One of the main challenges of designing with computa-tional tools is comprehending the relation between design and programming com-petences (Amiri, 2011), i.e. how parametric design manages to support creativity in the design process. Observing the designers' personal strategies during the process is one way to comprehend this relation.

Parametric design can be not only a support to realise 'analogue' morphological ideas, but also an important stimulus in the initial phase of concept design where it can generate variation by alternating not only dimensional parameters, but also topological relations between surfaces (Lee et al., 2013; Iordanova, 2007; Aish and Woodbury, 2005). By rapidly generating variations, the designer can explore morphologies that go beyond what could be generated by hand drawings, which is considered the conventional vehicle of ideation. However, automatically generating variations is not simply an aid to creativity, but it also helps to expand the limits of knowledge regarding what is possible (Liu and Lim, 2006), expanding therefore the design space, which is essential also for mass customization, as discussed pre-viously. Considering the popularity of the parametric approach among practitioners and (especially) students of architecture, researchers have many subjects to study the possible creative strategies using scripting tools, and to identify which are the most effective ones.

By nature, creativity and design attitude is difficult to frame; an attempt by Lee

(2014) is to analyze them through the so-called *Consensual Assessment Technique,* which is basically a jury panel that evaluates the results of the creative process according to some predetermined criteria, as well as through protocol analysis, which consist in discussing the creative process with the participants themselves.

With scripting languages that are integrated in modelling software, programming is becoming an integral part of design, enabling designers to adapt their working environment/tools to their creative needs, also by going beyond the pre-established ways of using their software tools. CAD-focused scripting languages can be integrated in the CAD software like Rhino, Blender, 3dsmax, Maya, or they can be open frameworks like Processing, ThreeJS, VerbNurbs; by learning them, architects and designers shift from the passive condition of tool users to the active condition of tool creators (Burry, 2013).

These 'tailor-made' design tools are (conceptually) connected also to the approach of the artisan: while governing software evolution, the developer/designer can gain an almost material-like sense of the software that is being shaped. As McCullough (1996) argues, the artisan's attitude can survive and flourish in the digital realm: when approached as just another material, Digital medium can guide the hand of the digital artisan to achieve the best possible outcome and a truly rewarding experience.

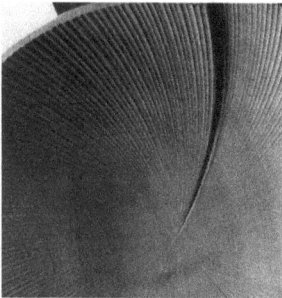

A bowl of David Pye, representing his concept of "workmanship of risk" - also applicable to the digital realm, as discussed

We can note another interesting connection between the apparent unpredictability of algorithmically generated forms and the concept of the 'workmanship of risk', a kind of artisanship *"using any kind of technique or apparatus, in which the quality of the result is not predetermined, but depends on the judgment, dexterity and care which the maker exercises as he works"* (Pye, 1968). According to this interpretation, parametrically designed and personalized products (realised with Digital Fabrication) can be seen as parts of the craft world and *vice versa*: the craft world can see parametric or algorithmic modelling as a frontier of innovation which brings it closer to the efficiency of serial production, in this case crafting code that achieves new aesthetic qualities.

As Maldonado (1992) predicts on a more philosophical level, *"despite the rudimentary level of its first applications, computer graphics have opened a new historic phase in the relation between thinking and perception: a new technical basis have been established to allow an operative (maybe even heuristic) relation between formal logics and visual modelling. However, this technical development won't cancel, as some might think, the old debate on meaning – on the contrary, it will reopen this debate with an even greater virulence"* (translated by V. M.)

3.6 Computational tools: three levels of abstraction

As we have seen, Computational Design implies a significant change in the creative possibilities and the creative approach required; but for the Product Design professionals or students who want to learn and practice personalizable design, also choosing the adequate software can be challenging; research literature with this scope is lacking. The author experienced such confusion first-hand while working on personalizable design projects; these led to the recognition that there are fundamentally different possible tools and workflows, each with their respective strengths and weaknesses. To illustrate these, we can use the following three projects, each object in close contact with the human body, but using Computational Design for various reasons:

(1) glasses: a functional product typology that performs a simple job, responding to low/medium mechanical expectations. The experimental project uses Computational Design to achieve a well-balanced shape in relation with the user's face, both for ergonomic and aesthetic motivations.

(2) shoes: a functional product typology with major complexity, requiring a flexible construction and higher mechanical performance. The experimental project uses Computational Design both for a novel aesthetic quality and for dimensional or material personalizability, enabled by rapid on-demand production.

(3) jewellery: a decorative product typology which, therefore, responds to minor mechanical expectations. The project uses Computational Design to create a personalization narrative by transforming a vocal message into a unique shape.[1]

Three products designed with computational tools on different levels of abstraction. Software screenshots on the next page.

These projects are not really revolutionary, as the practice of personalizable Computational Design for Digital Fabrication has already ventured into these product typologies, meaning that their personalizability is already proven and immediately comprehensible. Therefore, these can be considered good candidates for experimenting with the technical execution of personalizable design, without wandering into conceptual issues.

[1] This project was developed in collaboration with the start-up company Makoo Jewels; the author's role was the developing the online personalization algorithm, while the concept originated from the founders Giulio Galassi, Federico De Simone and Dario De Angelis.

The three projects imply different levels of computational complexity, hence varies the ideal design tool, each requiring a different level of abstract thinking:

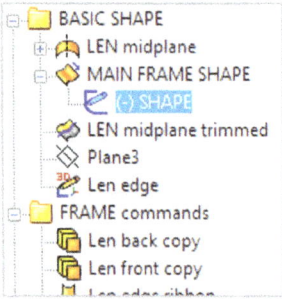

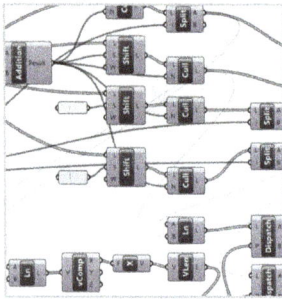

Screenshots illustrating the discussed three levels of abstraction, corresponding to the three projects on the previous page

(1) Low level of abstraction: solid parametric modeller (e.g. Solidworks, used for the eyeglasses frame). In this case the modelling process remains close to the conventional way: the model is defined through a series of steps, which are registered in a *model tree*. By carefully structuring this logical tree, the designer can predispose the model for personalization, although this must happen in a professional software environment, which cannot be handled by the typical end user. This fact suggests an artisanal business model, where an expert carries out the personalization in collaboration with the user.

(2) Medium level of abstraction: visual programming in a desktop software (e.g. Grasshopper, used for the shoes). In this case the modelling process is based on a conventional surface modelling software (Rhinoceros3D), but an additional toolbox is used to help automatizing the sequence of steps, particularly useful for repetitive geometries. Similarly to the previous case, we can modify numeric input parameters and the base geometry (e.g. curves). The Grasshopper interface allows performing various logical operations in a visual way, so it is relatively easy to approach also without advanced IT competences. This software can easily interact with others, so it's possible to develop user-friendly interfaces of personalization. This is possible both offline (Human UI) and online (ShapeDiver) through platforms which can create a bridge between the browser and Grasshopper, even though online performance remains limited because the updated geometry is streamed from the server; nonetheless, visual programming opens the possibility of a more ambitious business model with worldwide distribution.

(3) High level of abstraction: conventional web programming (Javascript with the ThreeJS library, used for the jewellery), which completely changes the modelling process. Textual programming requires a deep comprehension each step, the conscious handling of tens or hundreds of variables, as well as math skills for vector calculations and, finally, a lot of patience to trace back and solve all the emerging technical problems, which are made worse by browser differences and the con-

tinuously evolving web environment. Such effort can be justified by the resulting smooth(er) personalization experience, which is appreciable even for simple functional products, but especially important when personalization experience itself is a key value – rapid feedback is particularly beneficial when the design builds on a continuous flow of input data (e.g. voice) and user input has hardly predictable effects on the geometry. Direct textual scripting can enable the performance necessary for real-time (30 frame per second) animation. It's worth noting, however, that this kind of modelling is hard to practice directly: it is more convenient to start with a static model and/or a parametric one that requires a lower level of abstraction, like Grasshopper, which will then help to structure the software and obtain an engaging web application, thus enabling worldwide diffusion.

The evolution of computational tools can transform the designer into a contemporary artisan, who needs to develop the competences and experience necessary to work with the 'digital material', comprehending deeply how it works.

3.7 Blurring borders: design, craft, software
Designer and artisan

Digital Fabrication and Computational Design allow uniqueness and morphological richness which are values often associated with prestigious artisanal products, but recently we can observe a reconciliation of design with artisanship through new technologies. Historically, (Industrial) Design was born to support industry which have gradually substituted much of the artisanship, shifting attention towards fundamentally different values: the wellbeing of generalised groups of clients, replicating mechanically the best possible solution to a well-defined problem. Shiner (2007) seeks to clarify the true difference between artisanship, design and art through four distinctive characteristics: the artisan elaborates by hand (1) a specific range of materials (2) with masterful skills (3) to obtain a useful artefact (4); on the other hand, for design this latter is the only truly important one – interpreting freely 'useful' to include also cognitive functionality. But in the contemporary practice, Digital Fabrication often facilitates or substitutes both the manual work of the artisan and the processes of industrial production, gradually bringing the designer closer to the artisan's conditions. Therefore, it's possible to imagine a convergent evolution between designers and artisans, manifested in their similar effort to experimenting with forms, languages, functions and, potentially, with new ways of serving the user needs.

Obviously, the relation between design and artisanship has deep roots: the long-standing collaboration between artisans and designers is well-known. It is important, though, to distinguish between the many shades of artisanship, as the term has a rather nostalgic connotation, in an era when both traditional and industrial artisanship has dubious economical sustainability. As Micelli (2011) argues, there is a necessity of specialisation, and he identifies three possible approaches between translating artisanship, the creative artisanship and the adapting artisanship. The translating artisan completes designer activity, translating their 'vision' in proto-types; this relation is more like a partnership than a subordinate situation, different from the artisan who executes precisely the designer's project, that is typical in industrial production. Creative artisanship is characterized by the uniqueness of its achievements, which can be expressed in an artistic artisanship (maestros), but also in the experimental work at enterprises or research institutions which need advanced skills to prototype innovative products and technologies. Finally, Micelli describes adapting artisans, who personalize their products according the particu-lar preferences of the user – operating therefore with the same motivations as the already discussed mass customization. Opening artisanship towards creative col-laborations with other interlocutors can bring extraordinary value to the society: artisans are carriers of a professional culture with an extraordinary attention to de-tail and intrinsic motivation that pushes them to execute a high-quality work; their manual practice result in a tacit knowledge that can enrich the scientific-technical knowledge in various fields.

Digital artisanship and Makers

Therefore, as Sennett (2008) argues, the artisan's attitude is equally important for a long series of professions, from medical doctors to IT professionals. Indeed, also the digital world needs the attitude of an artisan who develops a deep knowledge of the given material (information), allowing virtuous modification and adaptation to client requirements – a particularly strong practice in the Italian context, where large software enterprises are rare (Granelli, 2010). So, there is an 'artisanal' way of performing digital innovation, even if this is substantially different from the con-ventional scientific or engineering way of doing innovation: while these determine a goal to achieve and adapt their tools to reach the predefined objectives, the artisans path of innovation is guided by the tools they have at hand, realising new things through the creative use of their resources, acting as a *bricouleur* – borrowing the term from Levi-Strauss (1962).

This attitude is a key feature of the Maker movement, which largely builds on the possibilities offered by the growing family of Digital Fabrication machines, mainly the low-cost models, with an ideology that is dominated by the democratisation of the access to the means of production. Digital production can be perceived as an industrial revolution, which acts against globalisation and brings closer design to the place of production and consumption (Anderson, 2012). Beyond technologi-cal evolution, the Maker movement itself made Digital Fabrication technologies more accessible, as well as hardware and software systems for sophisticated digital controls in manufacturing, and electronic components in general. Makerspaces and Fab-Labs have demonstrated that the effective use of these technologies is in reach for everyone; in fact, an essential component of the Maker 'rhetoric' is accessible tech education for both adults and the young. This contributes to a growth of readily available knowledge which could feed a renewal of artisanal (micro-)enterprises, especially combined with the financial incentives provided for Industry 4.0 in many countries. In order to raise competitivity in these enterprises, it would be desirable to create new functional and aesthetic qualities that were impossible to realise previously, according to the possibilities born from the intersection of tacit manual knowledge and digital innovations.

Software takes command

As already mentioned, the *bricoleur*'s approach is applicable also to the software world; a reason might be that digital resources are relatively easy to 'replicate' and modify, but difficult to develop from scratch. Therefore, software development tends to be 'opportunistic', trying to benefit as much as possible from already available resources and proceed as fast as possible, considering the intense competition that can rapidly render obsolete the results of a too slow development. Already developed software fragments constitute an important asset to recycle, which logically leads to an evolutionary process in a *bricoleur* spirit: rather than deciding a precise endpoint, a general direction is defined, and when development arrives to a crossroad, the seemingly most effective one is chosen. This approach is reflected in the widespread software (and business) development paradigm called *lean development*, which is based on the idea of releasing a *minimum viable product (MVP)*, to be developed gradually according to the feedback and further needs of the first users, maintaining the product eternally in a *beta* testing phase.

What is even more interesting from this book's perspective is that using Computational Design and Digital Fabrication, even physical products can become a question of software. Andreessen (2011) observes the invasive nature of software going as far as arguing that "software is eating the world", citing a series of 'hard' industries which have been turned around by software enterprises, capable of optimising dramatically the flow of resources, thus providing users with better products and services, faster and cheaper than ever. Therefore, just like software raised the possibility of unlimited mutations of 3D graphics 'inside' the computer, with widely accessible Digital Fabrication the same can be done to physical products, thus allowing not only functional and organisational improvement, but also a renewal of visual languages (Manovich, 2013).

Such a change of perspective, however, does not arrive intuitively to designers, but requires the conscious effort of elaborating not only "well-structured" digital drawings, but also valid concepts that resonate with the potential users' sensibilities; the next chapter will explore possible motivations for which users might feel tempted to choose a personalizable product over other serial options on the market.

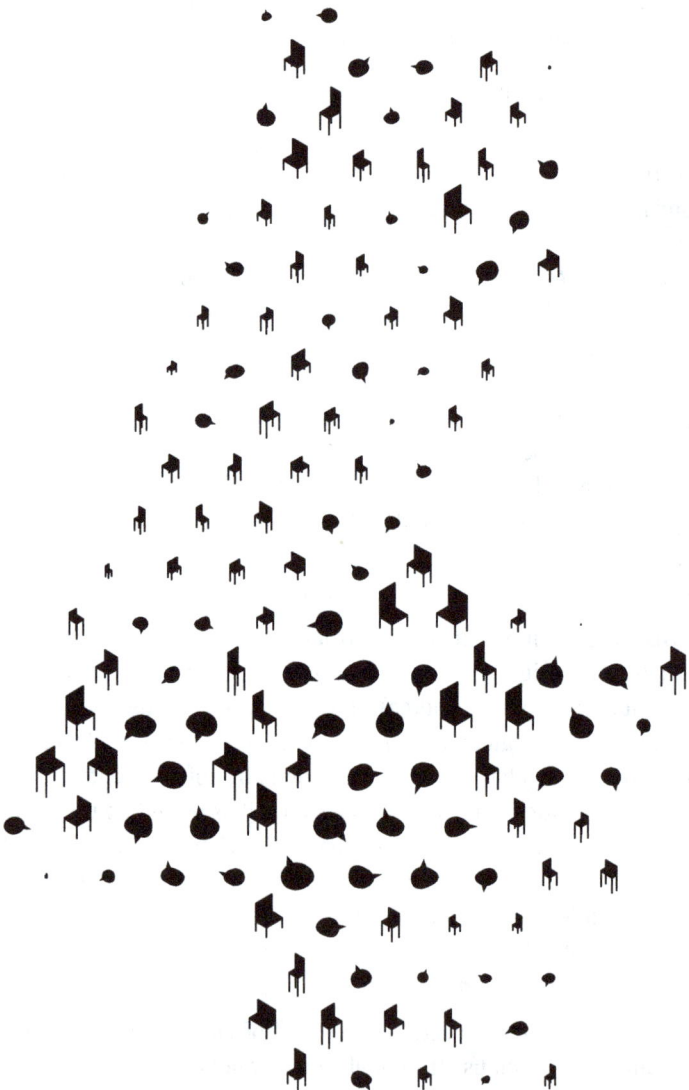

PART II
PRACTICES
CHAPTER 4
CASE STUDIES: PERSONALIZABLE PRODUCTS

While previous chapters explored various fields loosely related to the general topic of Open Design and Computational Design, this chapter starts focusing specifically on theme of the book: personalizable design. A series of case studies are analyzed, demonstrating best practices which use productively Computational Design and Digital Fabrication as means of creating products with flexible, user-modifiable form. The study of commercially available products helped to identify six recurring reasons which can motivate users to choose personalizable products rather than mass-produced alternatives, despite the typically higher cost, effort and time necessary to obtain these products. These six "variabilities" could be divided in two main groups: mechanical variabilities, which can motivate user intervention to improve the product's adaptation to physiology/ergonomics, to surrounding environment/objects or to functional/performance requirements. On the other hand, cognitive variabilities include factors such as aesthetic/emotional, social/cultural and narrative/experience personalization, adapting the object to the user's desires. The systemic organization of the dominant user motivations helped to develop a design method and a canvas tool for the strategic reproduction of these value propositions. The resulting Computational Concept Canvas is described in chapter 6 & 7, while its practical application is discussed in chapter 8.

Mapping motivations

Recently the software necessary to practice Computational Design become sufficiently accessible and easy to learn even beyond their original scope, architecture and engineering. As a consequence, we can observe a proliferation of products manufactured on demand which use Computational Design to offer qualities that are otherwise unobtainable with serial production. Our focus isn't so much on the aesthetic-morphological aspects, but it focalises on the changing relation between designer, product and user, offering these latter an increasing possibility to intervene in the definition of the products that surround them.

As of today, interactive Computational Design for product personalization is mostly applied on decorative products. Categories such as jewellery or fashion accessories naturally lend themselves to personalization, as these are chosen based on their compatibility with the user's personality – or, more accurately, these are based on and contribute to the (more or less consciously) constructed identity of the user. Today, in fact, the realms of social media promote the widespread practice of consciously cultivating and communicating identity, by sharing experiences and establishing personal style – a significant departure from the mass media age, when it was much easier to just adhere to values pushed by "professionals". The ease of the highly rewarding social practice of self-construction and self-promotion might have disputable long-term effects, but these are out of the scope of this discussion.

Personalization is far less present in "utilitarian" product categories. On the contemporary marketplace of industrialised societies, functional products face strong competition and their mechanical performance is under a scrutiny that leaves small room to sub-optimal resistance or material imperfections that are still common with Digital Fabrication. Much of the spending that goes into durable consumer goods end up paying for high-tech products, which are hard enough to manufacture affordably using the economies of scale, leaving small space for less efficient on-demand production. Similar considerations can be made on the other end of the spectrum: simple everyday products are available cheaply in countless variations, especially thanks to the efficient online marketplace. In-between, however, examples demonstrate that there are numerous ways of improving the mechanical performance of "medium complexity" products, especially if these need to be in close contact with the body or other objects.

Therefore, an overview of commercialised products with configurable shape has highlighted a number of reasons for which variability can be competitive, user motivations that are related to both mechanical and cognitive aspects. Both motivation groups could be divided in three, thus resulting six types of 'variabilities', of which it was possible to pinpoint one as dominant for each case study, as we will see on the following pages. The six identified types of variability (in two groups) are each identified by a couple of keywords:

Mechanical Variabilities:

- Physiology/Ergonomics – as human bodies obviously differ, the mechanical performance can be improved if a product is tailored to the relevant dimensions or shapes, for example through 3D scanning;
- Environment/Objects – products often need to fit in a specific built environment, or collaborate with other objects, extending or containing them, so better geometric fitting can optimise efficiency;
- Function/Performance – the available range of functionalities, use cases or performance can be personalized, both with a modular logic or completely new generative material qualities, either directly or through accessories.

Cognitive Variabilities:

- Aesthetic/Emotional – the simplest possible way of personalization, in order to better match the user's aesthetic taste and preferred emotional response;
- Social/Cultural – preferences can depend on belonging to specific social groups, either by choice, e.g. hobbies and music groups, or by origin e.g. ethnic cultures or sports teams;
- Narrative/Experience – various user activities can provide personalization data, or even the personalization itself can be turned into a memorable experience, if the designer constructs a specific narrative around it, e.g. souvenirs.

Many of the case studies allowed configuring various parameters that influence user perceptions on different levels, therefore it was necessary to evaluate the level of variability according to all six aspects for each case study. These evaluations on the 1-5 scale were organized in radar diagrams, present on each product sheet: the shape of the polygon depends on the characteristic combination of features, thus representing the profile of personalizability.

To explain the meaning of each kind of variability in a sensible, easy to understand way, the next pages will analyze three case studies for each. Beyond the evaluation of the variability and the synthetic description, there are further three key information regarding each project: Solution Space, Choice Navigation and Digital Fabrication; parameters derived from the three essential elements of successful *mass customization*, as discussed previously. The same criteria seem reasonable also for comprehending differences between our case studies, even if these are not diversified mass products, but products which were specifically designed around personalizability to be Computational *by Design*, and not by an afterthought.

Case studies overview

Mechanical Variabilities

Physiology/Ergonomics
Stan: a computer support to transform a normal desk into a standing desk
Wiivv: anatomic insole generated from the 3D scanned feet of the user
Feetz: shoes produced entirely with 3D printing

Environment/Objects
Highlight: a chandelier that illuminates the selected areas of the room
Parametric U-Hook: open source configurable hook to print at home
Makersleeve: user-assembled, configurable size protective sleeve

Function/Performance
Free Universal Construction Kit: connections between construction kits
MetaformTools: components to extend the functionality of space dividers
Nintendo Switch accessori: enriched gestures for game controllers

Cognitive Variabilities

Aesthetic/Emotional
Cell cycle: generative jewellery with wide margins for user intervention
EmotiveModeler: algorithmic generation of shapes based con keywords
Fitchwork: home accessories with configurable generative pattern

Social/Cultural
Hero Forge: hero figurines imagined for fantasy fans
Locatable: table with an incised map on the surface, position by choice
Minetoys: 3D print a selected fragment your world Minecraft world

Narrative/Experience
Copy Pastry: cookie cutter derived from a custom photo
Nicetrails: reproduce a landscape based on the GPS track of your hike
SketchChair: chair generated from a quick sketch of the user

personalization
for dominantly
MECHANICAL
aspects

personalization
for dominantly
COGNITIVE
aspects

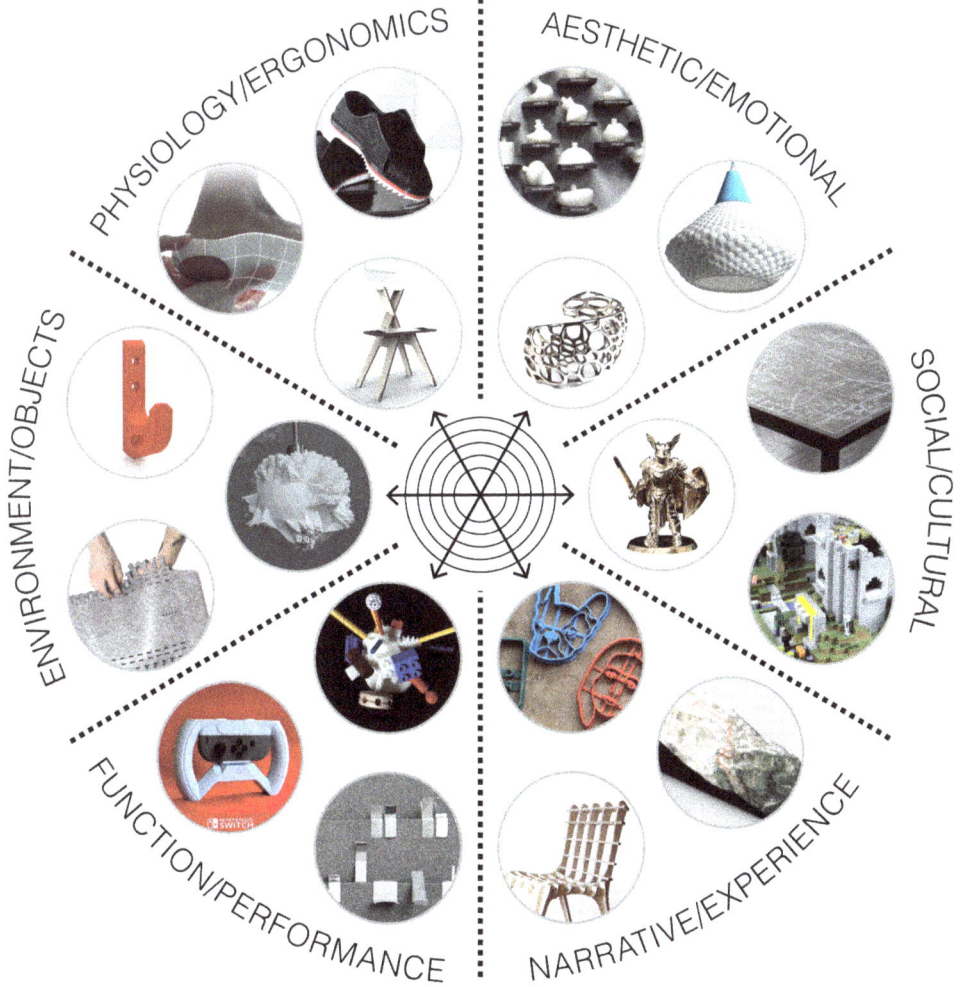

PHYSIOLOGY/ERGONOMICS

AESTHETIC/EMOTIONAL

ENVIRONMENT/OBJECTS

SOCIAL/CULTURAL

FUNCTION/PERFORMANCE

NARRATIVE/EXPERIENCE

Stan desk

Dominant Variability: Physiology/Ergonomics

Description: Stan is a computer support to place on a desk, allowing the comfortable use of a laptop while standing. Contemporary knowledge society requires the intense use of computers from many people, often eight hours a day. In the same time, there is an increasing awareness of the negative effects of the sedentary lifestyle, so there is a trend to change sitting desks to standing desks, which, however, is not easy to implement in already furnished offices. Therefore, Stan offers a variable height support for the computer and keyboard according to the physiological characteristics (height) of the user.

Solution Space: The possibilities of variation are limited to user height, material and graphics to engrave. The parametric model could be more articulated to enable a better adaptation to special kinds of computers, or to satisfy other functional needs.

Choice Navigation: The process of personalization happens through an extremely simple online interface. Actually, the project aims to demonstrate the proprietary online personalization technology of the company Twikit.

Digital Fabrication: laser cutting from multilayer wood and anti-slip felt

Designer: not specified

Web: https://www.twikit.com/standesk/

Wiiw insoles

Dominant Variability: Physiology/Ergonomics

Description: Wiivv substitutes the standard insole of whichever normal shoe, in order to improve comfort ant athletic performance. The product aims to relieve ortho-paedic problems which often lead to more serious prob-lems to the knees, hip or back. The product provides a better support both to the medial arch and to the heel, hence it competes with the performance of prescription insoles, but offers a more rapid and comfortable person-alization process at a lower cost.

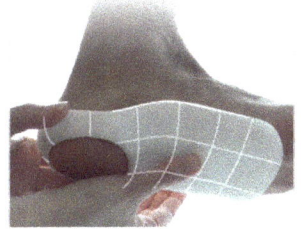

Solution Space: Variation possibilities are practically infinite, since the shape is adapted precisely to the 3D scan of the feet, using a smartphone app that identifies two hundred data points. On the other hand, visual dif-ferentiation is limited to the choice between a few pat-terns and colors.

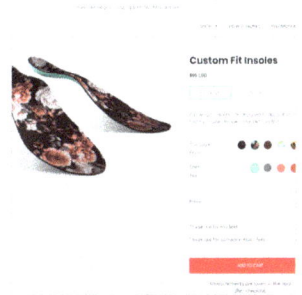

Choice Navigation: The personalization process hap-pens online, in two steps: the user first chooses a base model (normal or shortened) and the aesthetic proper-ties in the browser, then a dedicated smartphone app guides through shooting a series of photos from the ad-equate angles.

Digital Fabrication: SLS 3D printed nylon powder, coating in neoprene, details in silicone.

Designer: not specified

Web: https://wiivv.com/products/full-length-insoles

https://www.kickstarter.com/projects/wiivv/base-by-wiivv-custom-3d-printed-insoles

Feetz shoes

Dominant Variability: Physiology/Ergonomics

Description: Feetz promises the precise physiological adaptation of a wide variety of shoes of different style. On one hand this brand is far from being the first to experiment with 3D printed shoes, and it's not even the most advanced in terms of performance or aesthetic sophistication: exclusive models from Adidas, Nike or New Balance are far more interesting in this sense. However, Feetz was chosen as a case study because it is a brand entirely founded on the idea of (almost) completely 3D printed footwear, on demand, in short time. Although the brand's visual language is recognisable, it does not announce the production technology: the design remains discrete and it does not try to attract attention more than necessary.

Solution Space: Possibilities of dimensional variation are infinite according to the feet of the user. Currently there are seven available models (five for women, two for men) of essentially similar topology but different proportions. While it seems morphologically possible, the web interface does not offer a fluid transition between them, so it is still more similar to 'conventional' mass customization.

Choice Navigation: The personalization process can happen offline through a physical retail network, as well as online in two steps: first the user chooses the base model and the aesthetic characteristics in the browser, then a dedicated smartphone app guides the user in shooting a series of photos from the adequate angles.

Digital Fabrication: FDM printing with proprietary material in a pattern specifically developed for footwear requirements.

Designer: not specified

Web: https://feetz.com/

Highlight chandelier

Dominant Variability: Environment/Objects

Description: Highlight is a chandelier that personalizes the very act of illumination by letting the user choose what to illuminate in the room. The object starts from the reflection that living spaces widely differ by architecture, by furnishings, as well as by the way people inhabit them. Allowing the personalized distribution of light from a single source, Highlight can valorise the most attractive elements of the space (e.g. a painting on the wall) and facilitate activities in predetermined areas of the room. Beyond the elegant concept, the object features a sophisticated morphology, generatively co-designed by the user on a web interface by simply painting that light in the desired areas: a noteworthy difference compared to the context-less decorative approach typical to chandeliers.

Solution Space: Margins of variation are wide, but the rich and articulated morphology always follows the same, very recognisable visual language, which is personalized indirectly based on the illuminated areas.

Choice Navigation: Personalization happens in two steps: first the user scans the room with a special (borrowed) equipment, to be installed in the light socket. Subsequently the web application lets the user indicate which areas should be illuminated.

Digital Fabrication: SLS 3D printing in white nylon powder

Designer: Jussi Ängeslevä, Michael Burk, Iohanna Nicenboim

Web: http://highlight.digital.udk-berlin.de/

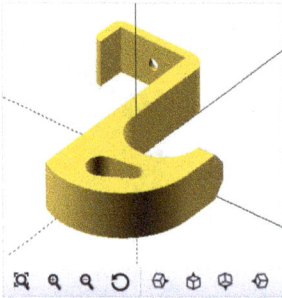

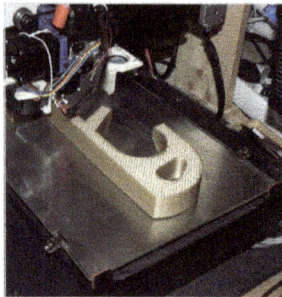

Parametric U-Hook

Dominant Variability: Environment/Objects

Description: Parametric U-Hook adapts its shape and dimensions to the situation of use and to the necessary load; product to be fabricated at home, on any 3D printer. The object does not offer particularly high performance beyond what's obtainable with mass products, it offers however the immediate availability of a 3D model for the specific requirements of the user. The project is open-source, therefore the user can configure the product and replicate the 3D model without limits. The design is spartanly functional, based on the designer's mission of codifying everyday objects to be spread freely.

Solution Space: There are wide margins of dimensional variation, as well as the possibility to change the topology of various parts of the design. Users can choose whatever 3D printing material and color available to them.

Choice Navigation: Personalization can happen both offline through the free OpenSCAD program and online through the Thingiverse platform. Using these free tools, the process is not particularly user-friendy, as it requires the comprehension of many parameters, rather than guiding the user through simple steps.

Digital Fabrication: optimised for FDM printing, even on cheap DIY models with the simplest PLA plastics. Possible to use anything else available.

Designer: Serge Payen

Web: http://sergepayen.fr/en/parametric-u-hook/
https://www.thingiverse.com/apps/customizer/
run?thing_id=1367661

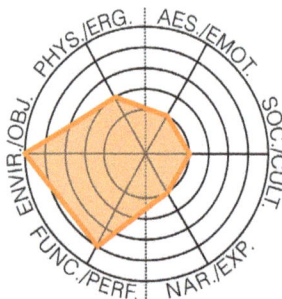

Makersleeve cover

Dominant Variability: Environment/Objects

Description: Makersleeve is a cover with adaptable dimensions for any smart device: phone, tablet, notebook. Since the dimensions of the rectangular object are fluidly variable, it can be adapted also to other objects, maintaining anyway the characteristic style of the author, who applies a similar construction technique also to his fashion work. As the name suggests, the Maker spirit is a fundamental part of the concept: the user has an important role in manufacturing. The cover arrives flat-packed and must be folded and mounted by the user – unless they ask the producer to do so, by paying a higher price. Anyway, the 'maker style' clearly dominates the visual language of the object, which proudly shows the construction technique.

Solution Space: Variations are limited to the color and dimensions of the cover.

Choice Navigation: The personalization process is extremely simple: the user chooses a color, the eventual request of assembly, and the device model or dimensions, inserting these choices in a simple online form. No preview is provided, as the parametric model is operated in the background, directly by the designer/producer.

Digital Fabrication: Laser cut felt in various colors.

Designer: Martijn van Strien

Web: https://www.makersleeve.com/

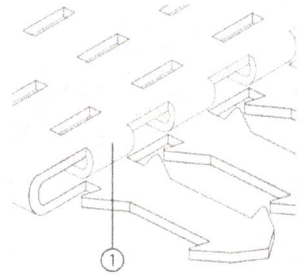

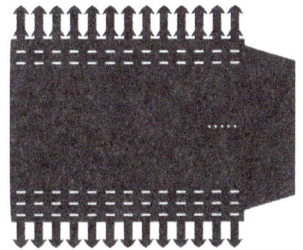

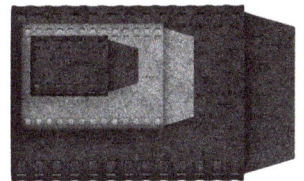

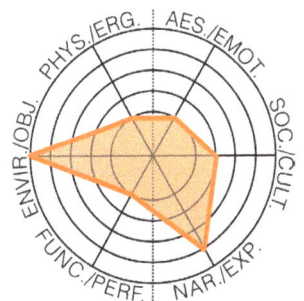

Free Universal Construction Kit

Dominant Variability: Function/Performance

Description: A kit of eighty adaptors, which enable interoperability between ten popular construction kits for children. Allowing to connect all these, the project encourages completely new interactions between otherwise isolated systems. This mutual extension of all the involved kits allows a radically new and creative type of hybrid construction play. Even if currently the connecting elements are not personalizable, the design builds on a kind of parametric thinking, that uses and valorises external data. The project was chosen to illustrate that pre-existing objects' functionalities can be extended with digital fabrication, giving a new, qualitatively different life to these objects.

Solution Space: Variation possibilities are limited to eighty (all possible combinations); therefore, strictly speaking this is not a computational model, but it is based on a computational (combinatory) logic. With a major effort, the idea could be implemented parametrically.

Choice Navigation: Rather than real-time parametric modelling, the user chooses between pre-baked STL files, released on various forums with Creative Commons license.

Digital Fabrication: The components can be reproduced with common, low-cost FDM 3D printers, as well as with more advanced machines.

Designer: The Free Art and Technology (F.A.T.) Lab

Web: http://fffff.at/free-universal-construction-kit

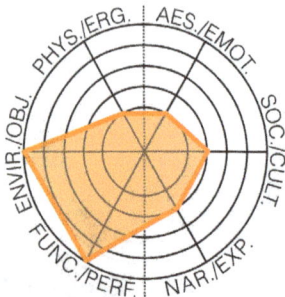

MetaformTools Accessories

Dominant Variability: Function/Performance

Description: Accessories to expand the functionality of the HermannMiller Metaform Portfolio, a system of office space dividers. The project starts with the observation that beyond the essential office equipment, people often surround themselves with other artefacts. MetaformTools aims to facilitate workspace personalization with additional functionalities which can be introduced, while maintaining the visual coherence. Additional elements were developed for 3D printing with the most accessible filament technology, which determines the obtainable design language, dominated by simple extrusions. It is possible to purchase both the physical product and the 3D model. Despite the use of simple form and a simple production technology, these products have an appreciable visual quality thanks to the use of exaggerated filament thickness, which is consciously valorised. Moreover, let's note how simple objects (space dividers) can obtain new functionalities through on-demand accessories.

Solution Space: Variation possibilities are limited and the design is not strictly computational, as a wide variety of combinations is pre-defined; however, the product hints the potential of variable functional extension.

Choice Navigation: The personalization process consists of the simple combination of shape and color.

Digital Fabrication: FDM 3D printing, either by the user or by the company; in this case, the especially thick layers characterize the print.

Designer: Studio 7.5

Web: http://www.metaformtools.com/

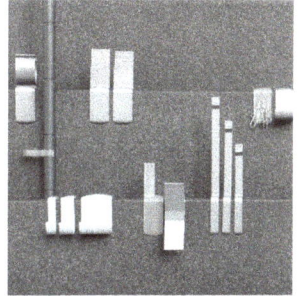

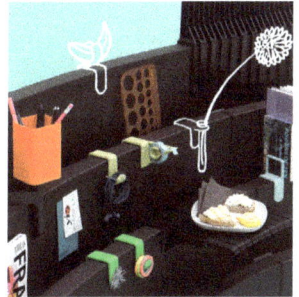

Nintendo Switch Accessories

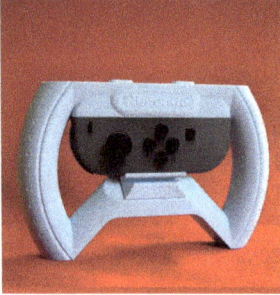

Dominant Variability: Function/Performance

Description: Accessories to enrich the Nintendo Switch game controllers, which feature a minimalist design that is not ideal for some of the videogames. To improve this situation, Maker communities have designed numerous accessories that can enhance game experience and performance by transforming the gestures of use, while maintaining the original technological contents. Later, even Nintendo itself embraced the idea with its Labo cardboard kit. These examples are not a truly parametric designs, but nonetheless good examples of how deeply accessories can influence a product's utility. The principle of functional personalization of electronic devices can be transferred to other fields, especially considering the growing movement of open hardware.

Solution Space: The possibilities of creatively extending the device varies on a wide range, but since this is not a strictly parametric model, we can only talk of potentials.

Choice Navigation: As mentioned, current models are not parametric, therefore only a simple choice is made.

Digital Fabrication: FDM 3D printing from the plastic of choice.

Designer: Helder L. Santos

Web: https://helderlsantos.com/portfolio/216/

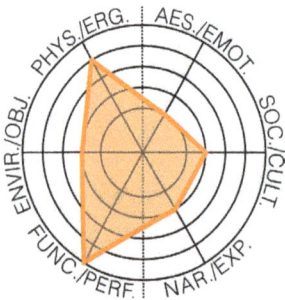

Cell cycle jewellery

Dominant Variability: Aesthetic/Emotional

Description: Cell Cycle involves the user in designing jewellery inspired by natural grow processes. A well-known classic of personalizable computational product design, part of a growing family of web applications which let the user to become a co-designer of fascinating objects inspired by nature. As most projects of the studio, the design is dominated by a rich pattern of interweaving elements.

Solution Space: There is a wide margin of aesthetic and dimensional variability, allowing also to shift between jewellery types. Aesthetic personalization can lead to distinct shapes, maintaining however the cellular structure which characterizes the design, thus maintaining also the authors (Nervous System) easily recognisable.

Choice Navigation: Personalization happens by modifying a basic model that features a uniform hexagonal cell structure. On one hand, the user can modify a series of parameters that determine the object's proportions and the grid density. On the other hand, one can intervene on the general shape through a series of control points and on the single cells that can be multiplied. A noteworthy complexity and sophistication can be achieved with a simple and fluid web interface, matured with years of improvement.

Digital Fabrication: available in various materials from SLS printed nylon to metals (lost-wax casting).

Designer: Jessica Rosenkrantz, Jesse Louis-Rosenberg

Web: https://n-e-r-v-o-u-s.com/cellCycle/

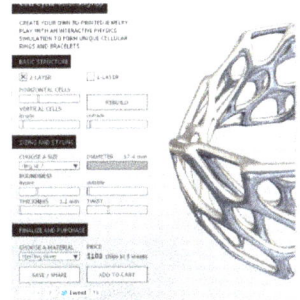

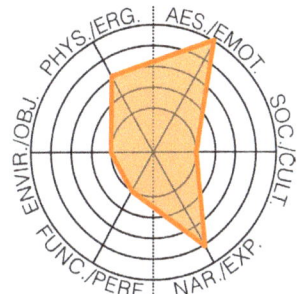

Emotive Modeler

Dominant Variability: Aesthetic/Emotional

Description: A research project that explores the possibilities of computationally generating product shape options starting from emotions the designer wants to stimulate. The project is based on the observation that any object's shape stimulates emotions on an unconscious level, and these emotional responses can be mapped to certain morphological characteristics. EmotiveModeler inverts the order: it utilises the emotive response as an input for a kind of computational modelling, which helps designers to explore a variety of possible morphologies in the initial design phase. For now, the project is more oriented towards the academic community of the design discipline, rather than the general public; however, using textual input could be an interesting approach also for providing a starting point for the parametric co-design of personalizable products.

Solution Space: Being a research project, possibilities are limited to modifying a simple bottle model. The object type remains unvaried, maintaining the division body/cap, while the shape changes significantly.

Choice Navigation: The parametric configuration process happens through a plugin developed for Rhinoceros3D.

Digital Fabrication: Prototypes were realised with stereolithography; however, in this case the material output is unimportant compared to the modelling process.

Designer: Philippa Mothersill, Michael Bove

Web: https://www.media.mit.edu/projects/emotivemodeler-an-emotive-form-design-cad-tool/overview/

Fitchwork product family

Dominant Variability: Aesthetic/Emotional

Description: A brand which offers a series of product of which the main characteristics is the rich, computationally generated pattern. The offered products have a simple and elegant base shape, that is 'cladded' according to user preferences. Available patterns are limited at the moment, therefore personalization is not particularly profound, but the approach of applying parametric patterns on simple base products could be interesting in other fields as well. The interactive implementation of the computational personalization is still missing, and probably will remain so in the near future due to the morphological complexity; however, it is a good example on how a computational visual language and moderate personalizability can help to establish a strong brand.

Solution Space: Variation possibilities are moderate, but the project scheme could easily allow further pattern or shape configuration.

Choice Navigation: Personalization happens through the choice between a few simple pattern and color options.

Digital Fabrication: The offered products are realised in numerous materials between plastics, porcelain and metals.

Designer: Travis Fitch

Web: https://fitchwork.com

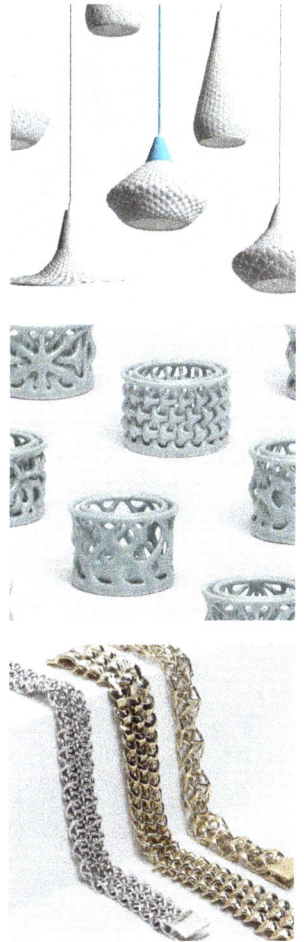

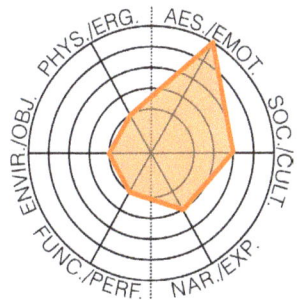

Hero Forge figurines

Dominant Variability: Social/Cultural

Description: Hero Forge allows fantasy fans (medieval, sci-fi, steampunk etc.) to imagine their heroes and materialise them physically as 3D printed figurines. This personalization service is based on the communities connected to imaginary worlds, populated by mythical personalities, with whom players can identify themselves. Hero Forge offers the possibility to further reinforce this connection through a physical manifestation of their avatars. These are configurable by choosing both the physiological properties and the characteristic accessories from a repository of hundreds of objects.

Solution Space: The margins of variability are extremely wide. Body proportions are fluidly modifiable and there are over 20 poses to choose from. The choice between hundreds of accessories generates countless characteristic combinations, even if these accessories belong to five main genres.

Choice Navigation: Personalization happens online through a 3D interface where the model can be modified in real time, visualising the object and a representative environment in grey. The configuration is intuitive despite the numerous options, thanks to the clear hierarchic organisation of the options that make the exploration even entertaining.

Digital Fabrication: SLS 3D printed plastic, stereolithography resin (for hand-painting), rough stainless steel, polished bronze

Designer: not specified

Web: https://www.heroforge.com/

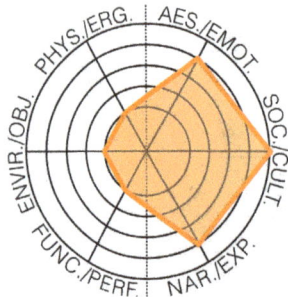

Locatable table with map

Dominant Variability: Social/Cultural

Description: A table on which owners can express their connection to a place on the globe. City plans have a considerable decorative value, but they can also declare a sense of belonging. As the eye runs through the map of a known city, one can remember past experiences on those streets. Locatable's concept is extremely simple: the user can choose any detail of the globe, which will be visualised on the surface of the table. The literally central role of a table in numerous activities suggests that this object could ignite conversations even among strangers. This reinforces the original social function of the table, going beyond simple decorations. The product was developed in the "Beyond Prototyping" research project.

Solution Space: Variations are limited to the surface of the table, where whichever detail of the world map can be engraved at any scale.

Choice Navigation: The online personalization happens through a simple search on the city to engrave; the user can move and zoom the map according to the usual gestures of Google Maps. Other basic properties such as table thickness or wood type can be selected as well.

Digital Fabrication: CNC engraving on wood, transparent resin filling.

Designer: Jussi Ängeslevä

Web: http://locatable.me/

Minetoys materialised game

Dominant Variability: Social/Cultural

Description: Minetoys offers Minecraft fans a way to materialise some of their digital creations. Minecraft is a videogame without a conventional narrative or pre-defined objectives, at least in its original version, which have attracted a fanbase of more than hundred million people. The game is based on the idea of constructing entire worlds from simple textured cubes; thanks to its simplicity, the creative experience is rather easy to approach, even without a particular design talent or technical competences. Minetoys benefits from the already existing community and demonstrates that web 2.0 contents can be valorised also in the physical reality. As far as visual style concerned, it is interesting to see that the native digital aesthetics of colored pixels continues to evolve even when technological constraints don't prescribe it anymore: exaggerated morphological simplicity highlights the narrative of the specific sub-culture.

Solution Space: Variation possibilities are limited so far: the main product is the personalizable Minecraft avatar. More complex scenarios can be reproduced as well, but the fragility of full-color sandstone printing limits the achievable level of detail. Choice Navigation: The online personalization consists of simply importing of the model from Minecraft.

Digital Fabrication: Full color sandstone 3D printing.

Designer: not specified

Web: http://www.minetoys.com/

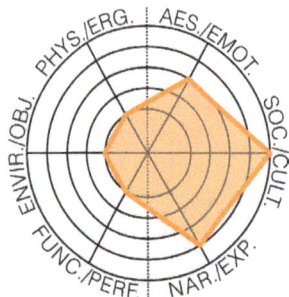

Copy Pastry custom cookies

Dominant Variability: Narrative/Experience

Description: Copy Pastry introduces a new playful element in the experience of home-made biscuits, as well as making special moment even more entertaining. The product started from the idea of reproducing realistic portraits in biscuit formats, which would be rather challenging with an artisanal method. Another possible application is catering at company events, e.g. reproducing the company logo in biscuit format, so food becomes an element of the brand identity. The principle of creating a narrative around a utilitarian object could work for other product typologies as well.

Solution Space: Variation possibilities are unlimited within the maximum volume of 15x10x1 cm. The contour and internal details are derived from the photo provided.

Choice Navigation: Personalization happens by submitting a photo on the website, along with eventual instructions regarding the areas of interest on the photo. The service has not been implemented as a computational design app, so the website does not show the 3D preview – predicting the resulting cookie needs an expert eye, which is too difficult to automatize. As human intervention is needed, Copy Pastry should be considered a kind of digital artisanship, where each order is processed 'by hand' in order to guarantee a satisfying result.

Digital Fabrication: FDM 3D printed plastic

Designer: Kriszti Bozzai

Web: https://copypastry.net/

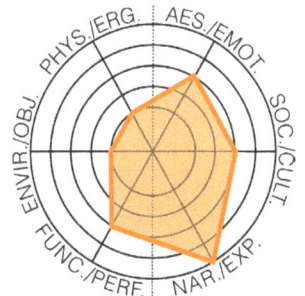

Nicetrails trekking trophy

Dominant Variability: Narrative/Experience

Description: With Nicetrails, excursionists can maintain a memory of the trail, as a kind of trophy, or prepare themselves from the next adventure... Maintaining a souvenir of past experiences is a habit of travellers, who can remember this way the best moments of the journey. Beyond the specific moments, for mountain trekking enthusiasts the entire trail is important, with its continuously changing perspectives and spatial complexity. The tracking of user activity during a memorable activity is a design principle that could be applied in a variety of contexts.

Solution Space: Variation possibilities are determined by the landscape to remember, which can be reproduced at different scales. Height can be modified also disproportionately in order to highlight better the spatial characteristics.

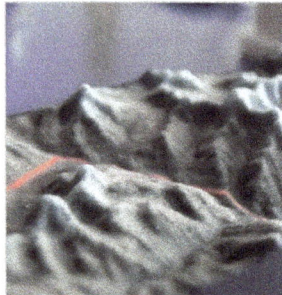

Choice Navigation: Personalization happens in the browser, loading the GPS (.gpx) coordinates that can come from trekking apps or specialised GPS gear. The online interface projects the path on a 3D model of the landscape obtained from satellite imaging.

Digital Fabrication: Multi-color inkjet 3D printing in sandstone.

Designer: Bernat Cuní

Web: https://www.nicetrails.com

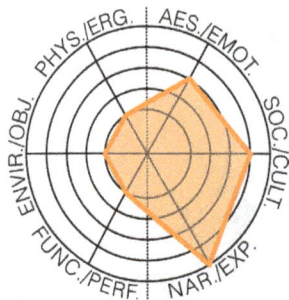

SketchChair diy seats

Dominant Variability: Narrative/Experience

Description: SketchChair offers the playful experience of designing a chair by simply sketching it on the computer screen. The offline application is free and open source, as part of a research project aiming to democratise product design, in this case simple structures constructed from a matrix of perpendicular joints. This enables designing also other furniture such as armchairs, tables or beds. Users obtain a production-ready file using the material and technology of their choice. The result of the creative experience becomes a part of everyday life, but also an object to be proud of, thanks to the underlying narrative of (computational) co-design.

Solution Space: There are wide margins of variation, since the user can design the profile without any particular constraints. In the same time, the reticular structure remains a recognisable feature of the project.

Choice Navigation: Personalization happens through an open source software available for Windows, Mac or Linux. The user first draws the chair by hand from the side view, then performs a virtual usability test thanks to a digital dummy which simulates the static and dynamic functionality of the chair.

Digital Fabrication: Any CNC driven cutting tool available to the user: typically CNC router or laser cutter.

Designer: Greg Saul

Web: http://www.sketchchair.cc/
https://www.kickstarter.com/projects/diatom/sketch-chair-furniture-designed-by-you

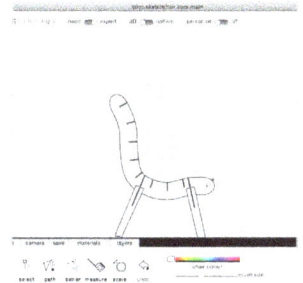

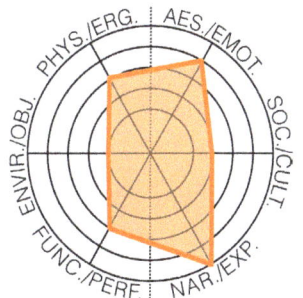

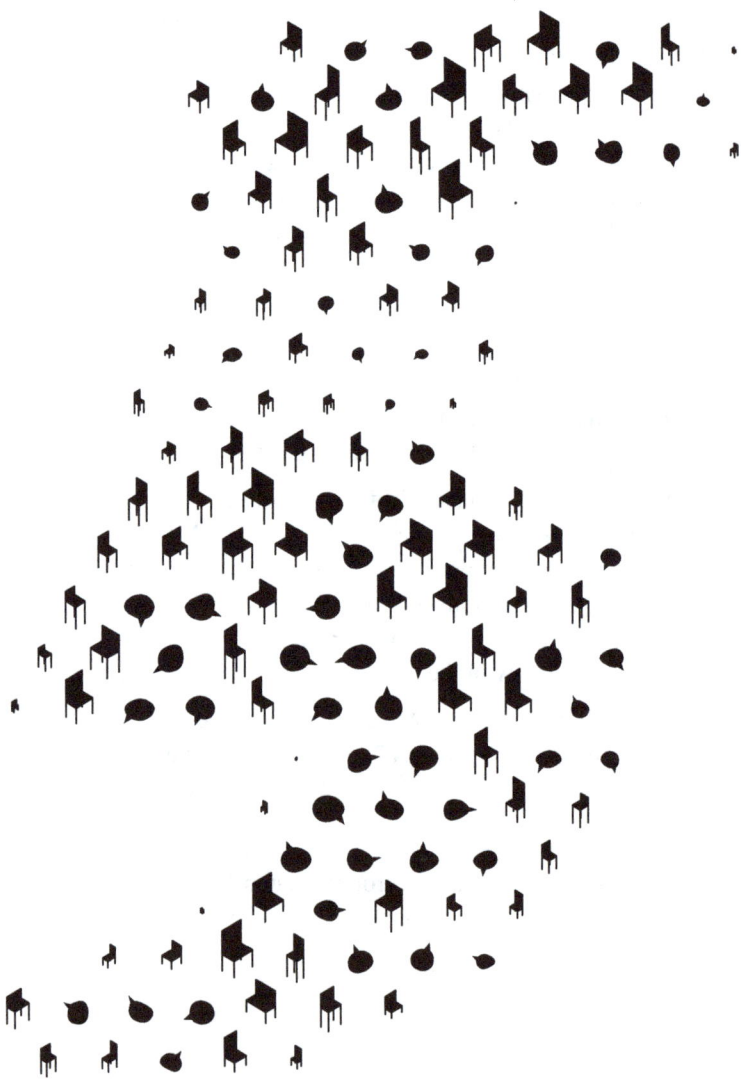

EVOLUTION / META-DESIGN

PART III
EVOLUTION
CHAPTER 5
SHIFTING DESIGN
TOWARDS META-DESIGN

After exploring Design's disciplinary evolution so far towards the productive use of computation for personalizable products, the third part of the book aims to promote the diffusion of this practice. Now there is a gap between the hopes and reality regarding the impact of Digital Fabrication in everyday life, and the reason for this could be (beyond technological limitations) a shortage of adequate competences on be-half of the Design profession, which has not yet found the right ways to valorise the new manufacturing opportunities, while respecting the still relevant limitations. Aiming at a literally 'human-centred' design, Digital Fabrication's major advantage seems to be enabling a better match between the user's desires and the product characteristics, i.e. personalizable design that enters in dialogue with every single user. This requires a design project with open variables and therefore a meta-designer who don't design a single object, but a multidimensional design space with an easy to use interface for the user/co-designer. Despite the rich scientific literature and many interesting experimental projects, personalizable products are still rare in the everyday environment; the book argues that designers could make a more conscious effort to widen strategically the range of personalizable product typologies. We suppose that personalizable product design could become a profitable niche design practice with consistent results, but beyond the 'computational' skills, it would require also a concept design approach which focuses on divergent user needs. Hence, the book proposes a new method for concept development, facilitated by the Computational Concept Canvas tool described in the next chapter.

5.1 A design shortage

As already discussed, Digital Fabrication has been long used for making special-ised equipment and precious tools for manufacturing; later it became available for relatively rapid and cheap prototyping and, subsequently, for sophisticated one-off pieces of art and design. Popular media as well as the Design profession received Digital Fabrication with great (but often naïve) expectations for its supposed revo-lutionary potential. However, the promising initial experiments were not enough to guarantee a widespread diffusion as a manufacturing tool. While access to Digital Fabrication tools is being democratised ever since the influential RepRap project (2005), so far they remained marginal as manufacturing tools of everyday products, so we are still a long way from diffuse on-demand manufacturing, which could help to avoid much of the wasteful overproduction, warehouses, intercontinental transportation and retail distribution, as enthusiastic Digital Fabrication promoters such as Neil Gershenfeld (2012) or Chris Anderson (2012) hope. It is no surprise that technological innovation can be interrupted after a brief phase of enthusiasm. If the first commercialised products happen to be disappointing, then it is usual to see a phase of recalibrating expectations, arriving gradually to a sustainable and productive use of the technology in question; the often cited (albeit approximative) graph of 'Gartner hype cycle' illustrates well this fluctuation of public opinion. As the so-called law of (Roy) Amara expresses, *"We tend to overestimate the effect of a technology in the short run and underestimate the effect in the long run."* In case of Digital Fabrication, if its products are not yet relevant in the everyday environment, performance or convenience are certainly limiting factors.

On the other hand, we should also suspect a shortage of the Design profession, which have not found yet the right ways to valorise these new production opportu-nities, respecting the still relevant limitations. Therefore, we can assert that beyond technological competences, there is a lack of conceptual competences which im-pedes the identification of the right areas of intervention where the characteristic advantages of Digital Fabrication could be adequately valorised.

5.2 Meta-designer and the value of choice

From a Product Design perspective, the book focuses on product variability accord-ing to the preferences and creative contributions of each individual user, as serving better these needs seem to be a possible evolution of the Design profession, which has gradually extended its attention from generic mass products to niche products for ever smaller communities. Producing personalized objects 'on-demand' for indi-vidual users is getting ever more affordable through Digital Fabrication, but it raises the need to produce efficiently the digital data for such differentiated production. As already discussed, Computational (or parametric, generative) Design can fulfill this need: a carefully structured mathematical model can adapt the geometry to the input from the users, who can intervene if there is an (easy enough) interface, thus adding to the designer's repertoire of approaches to serve divergent human needs.

Reflecting on the changes in the professional role, Jos De Mul (2011) argues that the designer *"should become a metadesigner who designs a multidimensional design space that provides a user-friendly interface, enabling the user to become a co-designer, even when this user has no designer experience or no time to gain such experience through trial and error."* This implies that creating an unforeseeable multitude of products requires a different approach compared to the design of a single solution. User diversity should not be circumvented but considered as an essential resource to create authentically personal artefacts. The profound trust in the creative capabilities of the (non-expert) user is fundamental also for design philosophies and practices such as Participative Design or Open Design. However,

> *One of the most important issues for open design is how much support and guidance is required to enable people to reach their maximum creative potential. The danger is that with too much structure the outcomes are controlled by the hidden hand of the designer and people are simply selecting from a range of options laid down by them. Too little support and many potential creative contributions are lost because starting from a blank page is difficult, even for experienced designers. (Cruickshank, 2014, p. 55)*

Personalizable design requires a significant shift of the design approach, a systematic work to understand what and how should be diversified. How would it be possible to go beyond marginal customization and raise significantly the value of the product, involving every single user in the design process? While we have seen interesting examples among the case studies, personalizable products are still rare among all products sold. Beyond technological limitations, we can think of at least two important reasons:

(1) Maybe the 'deep' personalization of everyday products is not particularly important for most people, considering the already wide variety of serial products. Actually, excessive choice introduces uncertainty in the decision-making process, thus diminishing sales and making consumers less happy about their choices; Schwartz (2004) calls this anxiety "the paradox of choice". Other studies found that such decrease in consumer motivation is not a universal phenomenon, but there is a strong fluctuation according to the specific conditions of choice (Scheibehenne, 2010). Anyways, as Pine and Korn (2011, ebook chapter 8) note *"customers do not want choice, they just want exactly what they want. Your job is to present the possibilities to them in a way that they can figure out what they want-even if they do not know what that is or cannot articulate it."*

(2) Moreover, the Design profession's current knowledge and practice might not be fit for the task of finding out which products should be personalized and how: designing products that are open to user interventions is an unusual problem for

Product Design, more comfortable with identifying a dominant necessity and satisfying it with a single solution. Ever since Designers emerged as distinct professionals in the beginning of the twentieth century, they were always intermediaries between industry and everyday life; sometimes introducing new technologies to the society, other times trying to resolve existing problems of the people; sometimes focusing on functional values, other times on symbolic values and meaning. In the present scenario, the profession includes an ever-increasing range of activities and goals, so it is difficult to pinpoint a dominant direction; nonetheless, in general we can observe a major sensibility to the design process that revolve around the users, examining their needs with a social vocation. This attention is manifested in numerous methods and tools, elaborated by both the academic community and design consultancies (e.g. IDEO), gathered in various web platforms and books.

However, the development of successful new products does not necessarily start from a predefined user group to promote. The client company often tackles with products in a specific typology or context of use, asking for improvement or redesign, thus requiring an inquiry across many segments of the potential market. Other times, the client does not have a specific product, but aims to valorise its knowledge, technological innovations or manufacturing resources – when a 'Technology Push' approach is necessary, to borrow a term form the business/marketing literature. In this situation, there is a solution searching for a problem, the opposite of the 'Market Pull' situation where the (target) customer's problem must be resolved with a product or service. There is a debate regarding the ideal starting point. Alexander Osterwalder, developer of the popular Business Model Canvas, argues that regardless the widespread belief, the development of a successful product innovation does not always start from a specific user; it is important, however, to finish with a product that helps users in their 'jobs', relieves their 'pains' and provide them 'gains' – to use the keywords of the Value Proposition Canvas. Emerges therefore the question: would it be possible to consistently widen the range of personalizable products that valorise Digital Fabrication and Computational Design?

5.3 Disseminating personalizable design

Considering the easy accessibility of the technical knowledge regarding Digital Fabrication and Computational Design, we can reformulate the previous question in this way: how would it be possible to promote the conceptual development of personalizable products according to the contemporary technological possibilities and user sensibilities? This book started from the assumption that Digital Fabrication can be valorised better through personalizable products using Computational Design. In search of the most effective action for developing personalizable products, we have observed that the technological competences necessary for modelling and fabricating personalizable products are already widely explored by the academic community, architects, designers, as well as Makers; much of these results are easily available online, and this knowledge is continuously updated on websites and forums. Therefore, wishing to contribute to the Design profession, we tackle with the problem of the creative act that brings to a variable project. In particular, there seem to be a lack of an adequate design method in the conceptual phase, which determine whether the resulting personalizable product will really meet divergent user needs, or it will simply make the choice more frustrating.

Hence, we assume that the development of personalizable products can become a consolidated practice with consistent results, but it requires a concept design approach which is more sensitive to divergent user needs. Therefore, focusing on variability, the next chapters propose a new concept design method, that derives from the experience of various projects, workshops and didactic experiences. These led to the development of a paper-based tool, a canvas to guide the thinking process from the choice of product type towards a product concept, of which personalizability is a distinctive feature. On the long term, the proposed approach might enrich the Design profession with new creative competences, that could help not only to provide more desirable products to the user, but also to valorise their creative potential in the process of personalization.

> *"The past few centuries have given us the personalization of expression, consumption, and computation. Now consider what would happen if the physical world outside computers was as malleable as the digital world inside computers. If ordinary people could personalize not just the content of computation but also its physical form. [...] Industrial production would merge with personal expression, which would merge with digital design, to bring common sense and sensibility to the creation and application of advanced technologies."* (Gershenfeld, 2005, ebook 13%)

5.4 Design methods and tools: which one to choose

As discussed, in a future scenario of increasingly sophisticated technological opportunities, it is equally important for designers to comprehend the conceptual opportunities. This book is geared towards new methods and tools that could be useful for the design practice, as well as for the education of a new generation of designers.

Facing the increasing complexity of the problems tackled by the Design profession, John Chris Jones (1970) have identified two main approaches to carry out the creative process, arguing for the "glass box" as the right metaphor for the professional designer's work – as opposed to the "black box" approach which mythicises the creative process. Or, even better than the "glass box", Jones speaks of the designer as a "self-organising system" between these two extremes. From that pioneering era which have founded the conscious discourse on the methods and tools of design (see also the Ulm School, 1953-68, or Jones and Thornley, 1962), the discipline tried to evolve the idea of transparently managing the creative steps through many methods

Illustration of the difference between design approaches "black box", "glass box" and "self-organising system" (Jones, 1970, pp. 46, 50, 55)

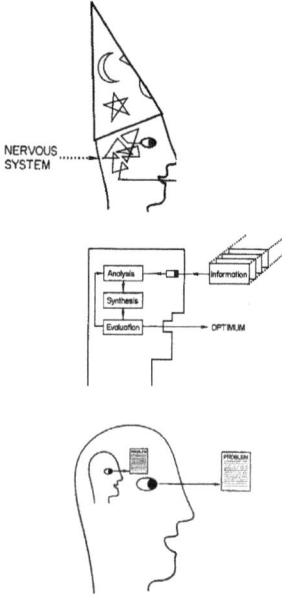

and tools based on many underlying philosophies and psychological models. For example, design consulting firm IDEO uses a series of paper-based tools to make its research activities more effective through interdisciplinary collaborations, which led to a widely recognised capacity for innovation of products and services. Its key figures are promoters of the so-called Design Thinking (Brown, 2009), that is the application of creative strategies on a wide range of situations, also beyond the conventional limits of the (product) design profession. They also argue that the designer's approach can donate a "creative confidence" to people who wouldn't consider themselves creatives (Kelley, 2013). More importantly for our discourse, IDEO shows how to divulgate a design attitude through the distribution of simple tools that facilitate different phases of the design process, which they divide between inspiration, ideation and implementation (http://www.designkit.org; IDEO, 2015). The ample non-designer public they target determines also the simplicity of the tools, which are well illustrated and self-contained, with brief descriptions for each step, posing questions that are open for creative re-interpretation. IDEO underlines that the proposed mindsets, methods and tools are only suggestions to choose from, according the problem at hand and the sensibilities of the team. On the other hand, this book focuses on a more specific area, the evolution of Computational Design through personalizable products, seeking their place in the material culture of the future. Therefore, from the ideal method/tool we expect to facilitate the process of transforming a static design project into a dynamic one, according to the specific possibilities of Computational Design and Digital Fabrication. This is a peculiar requirement from a design tool; an examination of contemporary design method collections (e.g. Martin and Hanington, 2012; Visocky O 'Grady and Visocky O 'Grady, 2006; Tassi, 2008; Kuma, 2012) haven't led to discovering any particularly well-fit tool for the purpose. There were, however, some inspiring examples:

- Personas: synthesis of the user research in invented representative users;
- Kano Analysis: evaluating the impact of product attributes on user perception;
- Key Performance Indicators: exploring different expectations;
- Lotus Blossom Idea Generation: expansive analysis of a design challenge;
- Value Proposition: evaluation according to jobs, pains and gains;
- Customer Journey Map: mapping of use phases and situations;
- Evaluation Matrix: systematic comparison of numerous alternatives.

The proposed new tool focuses on the conceptual development, with a special attention on the crucial initial phase of problem finding, called also "the fuzzy front end of innovation". Trying to eliminate this fuzziness, the often-cited Koen et al. (2001) have examined the development process of new products in various companies, identifying a model composed of five steps: opportunity analysis, opportunity identification, idea genesis, idea selection and conceptual and technological development. These are rather generic steps, but anyways it is a useful division that is reflected in the proposed design tool.

Speaking of the formalisation of the design process, we should be careful about designer sensibilities; formal approaches can be difficult to apply, but particularly beneficial when working on problems that are almost impossible:

> *Within the industrial design community there is some mistrust of formal approaches that do not exactly match the designers' requirements. However, in the same team there may be individuals who can take comfort from well-defined approaches during the stressful concept creation process when the results are on the borderline of being achievable. Therefore, the methods should be clearly defined to give the guidance needed, but at the same time they must be transparent in order to ensure that using the method does not become the primary focus of the work. The method should allow the team to follow the approach, but at the same time let the team and its individual members focus on the content of the project. The method must support the process without focusing too much attention on itself. Keinonen (2006, pp. 45-46)*

One tool that follows this approach is, in fact, already widely used in companies: the Business Model Canvas of Osterwalder & Pigneur (2010) provides a well-defined structure to the ideation and evaluation of the entrepreneurial model, stimulating the canvas user to consider a series of factors that are fundamental for the development of a profitable product or service. The canvas format offers a logical disposition of communicating elements and plenty of empty space to be filled with post-its. This format turned out particularly effective in countless environments, from start-ups to large enterprises. An offshoot of Business Model Canvas is the Value Proposition Canvas (Osterwalder et al., 2014): an even simpler format that stimulates an articulated discussion on the perceived value of the product beyond the openly declared functionality (jobs), investigating also difficulties (pains) and benefits (gains) from the perspective of various user profiles. Similarly to the Business Model Canvas, the proposed tool (detailed in the next chapter) aims to provide a flexible but uniform structure to the analytical observations and to the design ideas, helping a comprehensive development by reminding the designer to consider a range of important factors that could underpin the success of a personalizable product, as well as the possibilities of Computational Design and Digital Fabrication.

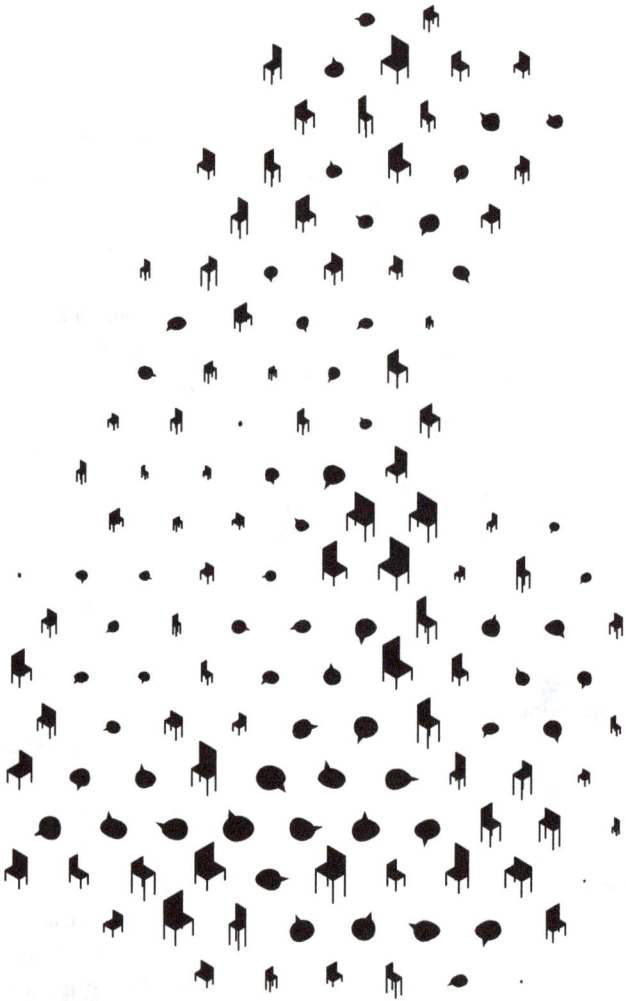

EVOLUTION / CANVAS

PART III
EVOLUTION
CHAPTER 6
COMPUTATIONAL CONCEPT CANVAS: A DESIGN TOOL

As we have seen in the previous chapters, offering personalizable design requires a special attention, not only on the technical, but also on the conceptual level. While technical knowledge regarding Digital Fabrication and Computational Design is already widely available, it is still challenging to identify viable opportunities and to develop valid concepts. Based on the assumption that personalizable projects would benefit from a specialised design approach/method, a Canvas tool was developed, which is described in detail in this chapter. The Computational Concept Canvas is a tool to help the conceptual development of meaningfully personalizable products. It is structured specifically to facilitate opportunity identification and conceptual design, based on a set of key advantages (variabilities) derived from numerous case studies of existing personalizable products realised with Digital Fabrication. Apart from this central module, the canvas helps the initial analysis of the product typology and the final detailing and illustration of the design concept. This chapter introduces to the workflow and structure of the canvas, while the next chapter gives step by step instructions for compiling each of the 12 fields, organized in 3 modules.

6.1 Objectives and target

We assume that the current knowledge and skills (and therefore practice) of the Product Design profession is not reliable enough for finding the product categories where personalization would be desired, and then develop well-balanced products that can cover unmet needs. Designing a product that is open to the user's modification (before production) is an unconventional problem for a product designer, more used to identifying a dominant need and to satisfy it with a single solution.

Personalizable product design is significantly more complex than 'static' product design: while it is still necessary to design a functional and desirable base model, an additional effort must be invested in developing an adequate solution space and choice navigation system. Apart from the conceptual complexity, it is far more difficult to create the parametric model of the dynamic geometry than 3d modelling of a 'static' product. Therefore, it is important to have an early understanding of why the user would choose a personalizable product, which are the desirable degrees of freedom and what constraints the 3D design must respect.

The "Computational Concept Canvas" was built with the assumption that a visual format helps to keep in mind all the critical issues, trace the design progress and make different ideas easy to confront. The CCC is a canvas template (available in different sizes) that contains a series of fields which leads and documents the conceptual design phase from the choice of a product typology to the definition of the value offered and the main morphological and technological characteristics of the product. The output of the canvas is a concept ready for implementation in a 3D modeller, to be followed, as usual, by prototyping and the subsequent steps of commercialization.

On one hand, the Canvas targets professional designers and organisations, primarily those already possessing the necessary Computational Design knowledge and/or Digital Fabrication equipment to valorise, searching potential application fields. On the other hand, the tool aims also Product Design students, who will have the bulk of their career in a future with an extremely saturated marketplace, where (as we hypothesise) one of the possible ways to stay competitive will be to satisfy the most particular individual needs using the ever more powerful and sophisticated technical tools.

6.2 General structure

Therefore, the logical structure of the Computational Concept Canvas (CCC) tool was derived from its objective of guiding the design process from the choice of a product typology to the concept of a variable product. To do so, the Canvas offers a series of fields for the analysis according to numerous aspects. The most relevant of these come from the already discussed case studies, which were categorized according to the variabilities that determine the perceived value of the products.

Based on these, the backbone of the work on the canvas is the examination of the chosen typology according to the 6 variabilities that could make the personalization desirable:

- Mechanical Variabilities:
    - physiology/ergonomics;
    - environment/objects;
    - function/performance.
- Cognitive Variabilities:
    - aesthetic/emotional;
    - social/cultural;
    - narrative/experience.

Moreover, there are 3 additional factors that determine the feasibility of the personalization using the available Computational Design & Digital Fabrication tools:

- Manufacturing Requirements:
    - material/mechanics;
    - shape/structure;
    - special components.

To each of these 9 factors, there is a corresponding quantitative question, that asks to evaluate approximately how much the relative user requirements determine the design; current diversity within the given product typology can strongly indicate whether there are divergent requirements, but designers should consider also the possibility of currently unmet needs. High evaluations indicate greater probability of developing concepts that are personalizable according to the given parameters.

While this system of criteria is the backbone of the analytical work on the CCC, it is completed with already existing frameworks and visual tools, such as the mentioned jobs-pains-gains analysis from the Value Proposition Canvas, the widespread personas technique, moodboard, or storyboarding of the customers journey.

The related fields on the canvas are laid out in an approximate reading order, from left to right, from top to down. It was not possible to establish a strictly linear order of execution, but this can be considered normal, as non-linear interdependencies can easily occur in real life projects as well. It is important, though, to maintain the proximity between the interacting elements, and this principle was respected as much as possible when designing the CCC.

6.3 Logical modules and process

The 15 fields of the canvas are grouped in three modules, which should be completed sequentially: even if fields within the module A and B are not compiled in strict order, the designers should fill in at least a hypothesis of them before moving on the next module.

Module A. Product typology definition (left)

A1. deciding the product typology, i.e. adequate scope of the design activity;

A2. analysing existing products within the chosen typology (benchmarking);

A3. clarifying the possible user values through jobs-pains-gains analysis.

Module B. Personalization principle definition (center)

B1. evaluating possible personalization principles and personalizable features;

B2. constructing personas to represent potential users and personalization needs;

B3. identifying design opportunities between B1 and B2.

Module C. Detailed concept definition (right)

C1. analysing manufacturing requirements and identifying reasonable options;

C2. collecting morphological references (moodboard);

C3. crystallising the product concept based on previous opportunities;

C4. distinguishing between variable and invariable elements of the design;

C5. defining the personalization process through storyboarding;

C6. hypothesising personalization outcomes based on the three personas.

6.4 Alternative formats

In order to maximize the utility of the proposed tool in a variety of contexts, several versions have been elaborated in different dimensions, for individual or group use, with or without post-it notes, allowing both continuous development (post-its on big canvas) or rapid iteration (direct writing on small canvas). The entire toolkit is available for download with Creative Commons license, complete with a detailed user guide.

Normal canvas: canvas for working in groups, using standard post-its (3x3" or 76x76 mm). Canvas dimensions: 1490x640 mm, foldable to A4 format for portability.

Small canvas: canvas for individual work or small groups, using small post-its (2x1.5" or 52x39 mm). Canvas dimensions: 1000x360 mm, foldable to 200x360mm.

Compact sheet: mini-size canvas for individual work, for direct writing on the sheet. Dimensions: printable both A4 or A3, for cheap printing to stimulate iterations. For convenient writing in the restricted space, the small sheet contains a vertical (rotated) version of the canvas with simplified graphics. Available with or without text instructions on the sheet itself, the former as reference only.

Triple sheet: mini-size canvas for individual work, cut in three pieces for convenient handling. Dimensions: print recommended on A4 sheets (3x), suitable also for A3 sheets. Offers slightly more space than the compact sheet and instructions for all fields are included on the first sheet.

Regardless the format, all versions of the canvas share the same fields, which are coded with a letter-number combination (e.g. C5); the suggested contents of all main fields are described in detail in the next pages in the recommended order of progress.

A2 BENCHMARKING	B1 DESIGN VARIABILITY B1 MECHANICAL / COGNITIVE ASPECTS	C1 MANUFACTURING REQUIREMENTS	C5 PERSONALIZATION PROCESS
A1 PRODUCT TYPOLOGY	B3 OPPORTUNITIES	C3 PRODUCT CONCEPT	C4 COMPONENTS OF THE PRODUCT
A3 USER VALUE	B2 PERSONA 1 / B2 PERSONA 2 / B2 PERSONA 3	C2 MORPHOLOGICAL REFERENCES	C6 PERSONALISED PRODUCTS

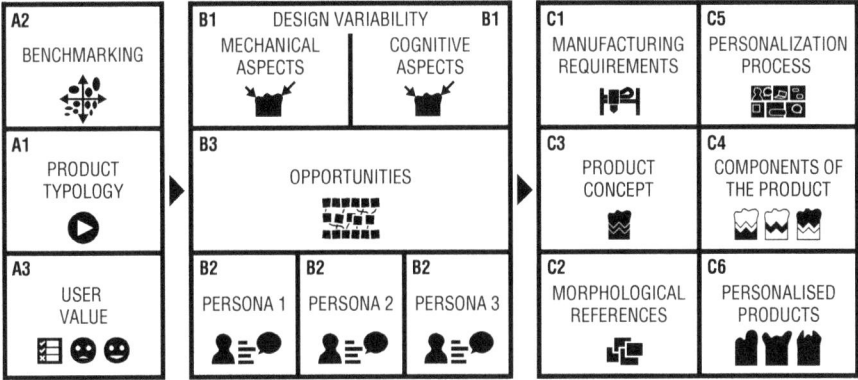

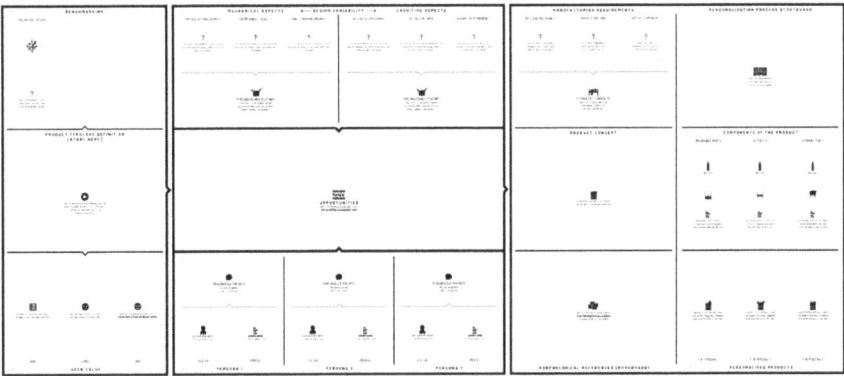

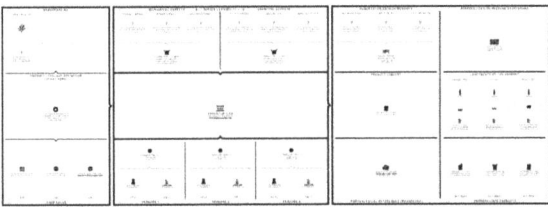

Top: logical scheme of the canvas, as outlined in section 6.3 and discussed in section 6.5.

Bottom: All formats of the canvas as described in the section 6.4. Illustrated proportionally; standard A3 and A4 sheets in the bottom row, large scale prints on the top.

For printable PDF versions of the canvas, please visit www.computationalbydesign.com

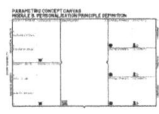

6.5 Workflow overview

Module A. Product typology definition

A1. Product typology definition. The starting area where the designers enter the product typology that they want to redesign for Digital Fabrication, aiming for a personalization as a key competitive advantage.

A2. Benchmarking. Exploration of the current variety within the chosen product typology, through a set of examples organized according to observable tendencies. The benchmarking should highlight how much divergence is there among currently existing products in the category, hence indicating the already existing need for personalization.

A3. User value. The third square in the bottom with the title 'Usage' helps to clarify the product typology's "reason for being" by analysing the jobs users want to carry out with the product, the pains (difficulties) they might experience during the usage and the gains they hope to obtain as a result.

Module B. Personalization principle definition

B1.1 Design Variability. Area of key importance, where the designer analyzes how much the previously mentioned 6 variable aspects (derived from case studies) determine the shape, usage and perceived value of the product. Each of these aspects are evaluated on a 1 to 5 scale according to a specific question, and the motivations are registered on a post-it note. This field relies on the capacity of the designer to critically assess the design of existing products, building on the observations in the previously filled fields of the canvas (A2. Benchmarking and A3. User value).

B1.2 Personalizable features. In this field the designer should clarify how the most interesting variable aspects (evaluated in B1.1) might influence the design of the features of the product, respecting the given typology's functional requirements. This field should clarify which part(s) of the product can be personalized while satisfying the requirements of the given product typology. According to the previous evaluation (on the 1 to 5 star scale), the most interesting aspect(s) should be considered, while dropping those with low ratings.

B2.1 Personas Profile and avatar. In order to comprehend whether user needs are sufficiently divergent to justify a personalizable product, in this area the designer constructs 3 'imaginary' user profiles according to the widespread personas technique. To create empathy and allow quantitative work, fictional personal details and an evocative avatar (drawing or photo) are added, making the persona a realistic character for whom to design. The constructed personas should have markedly different expectations from the chosen product typology.

B2.2 Personalization need. After constructing the personas, in these fields the designer should insert ideas regarding their most particular needs, which would motivate them to engage in a personalization process.

B3. Opportunities. In this area the designer should connect the possibly personaliz-able features (B1.2) with the identified personalization needs (B2.2). The ample and unstructured space is open for idea generation, allowing to dedicate the neces-sary number of post-its for ideas, ideally connected to previous observations; con-nections should be marked e.g. with sticky paper tape. The designer should try to identify which personalizable features have the strongest connections to the identi-fied personalization needs, resulting in more defined ideas about the desirable con-figuration and morphology of the final product. However, in this phase it is not yet necessary to define precisely the product concept, it is more important to map out many opportunities and focus on connections.

Module C. Detailed concept definition

C1.1 Manufacturing requirements. Approaching the final concept, the designer analyzes the requirements that determine the feasibility of the previously identified product/feature opportunities, trying to find the ideal Digital Fabrication strategy. For the ease of discussion, the manufacturing requirements are divided according to three aspects; similarly to the nearby B1.1 fields, beyond the verbal assessment the feasibility of these aspects should be rated on a 1 to 5 scale, where lower ratings indicate harder to satisfy requirements, which need extra attention.

C1.2 Technology candidates. In this field, the designer should identify which digital fabrication technologies could match the above requirements. Beyond the digitally manufactured components, the product might include parts which must be realized with conventional, serial manufacturing technologies; these requirements should be listed as well.

C2. Morphological references (moodboard). This field illustrates the expected vi-sual qualities of the final object through a collection of images and/or text descrip-tion. The morphological references (moodboard) should be coherent with the range of previously constructed personas (see the neighbouring B2 fields).

C3. Product concept. This field contains the morphological concept of the product, considering an 'average' personalization. Based on the previous analytical work and ideation, the overall design should be illustrated, as detailed and precise as pos-sible, providing a preview of the final product.

C4. Components of the product. Further illustrating the concept outlined in the C3 field, here the designer should distinguish between the variable and invariable parts of the design, highlighting also the interface where they meet. 'Variable' parts are those which can be personalized through parametric design, to be manufactured with digital fabrication. 'Invariable' parts are those which cannot be personalized, either because they need to have a given geometry in order to function properly, or because personalization would not change the object's perceived value. Invariable parts can be produced by either digital fabrication or serial production. Finally, under 'interface' the designer should describe where/how variable and invariable parts meet.

C5. Personalization Process Storyboard. This field contains an illustration and description of the main steps necessary to obtain the custom product. Based on one of the previously constructed personas, the storyboard should begin with the emergence of the personalization need and proceed with the persona entering in interaction with the system of personalization, e.g. webpage or physical shop.

C6. Personalized Products. This field should illustrate and describe briefly three hypotheses of the product, personalized for the three previously constructed personas (B2). Noteworthy differences in the creative input should be described.

Workflow conclusion and next steps

To conclude the description of the of the different areas of the canvas and the related steps, it's worth noting that the process is not necessarily linear, because emerging ideas could stimulate some review of the previous steps. In fact, when the canvas is completed, it is advisable to review it entirely in order to confirm whether the previous statements are still valid and whether they are coherent and supportive of the elaborated concept. The result of the work could also be the rebuttal of the original hypothesis of working on the chosen product typology, especially in an entrepreneurial environment, where working on sub-optimal ideas can have substantial cost, whereas in didactic settings wild ideas can yield even better creative development. Regarding the timeframe, considering the previous experience, it would be advisable to dedicate 4-5 days for a full and accurate compilation of the full canvas with a working group. Naturally the growing experience or the autonomous work on a compact version canvas would decrease the time necessary for arriving to a valuable conclusion. As a result, the designer can expect a concept that is mature enough to kickstart the demanding phase of computational modelling, with a confidence about the potential utility of the personalization.

The described Computational Concept Canvas tool provides a framework only for the first steps of a design project. The subsequent step is to elaborate a parametric model which allows the user to customize the product in an adequately large solution space, according to the degrees of freedom that were outlined previously.

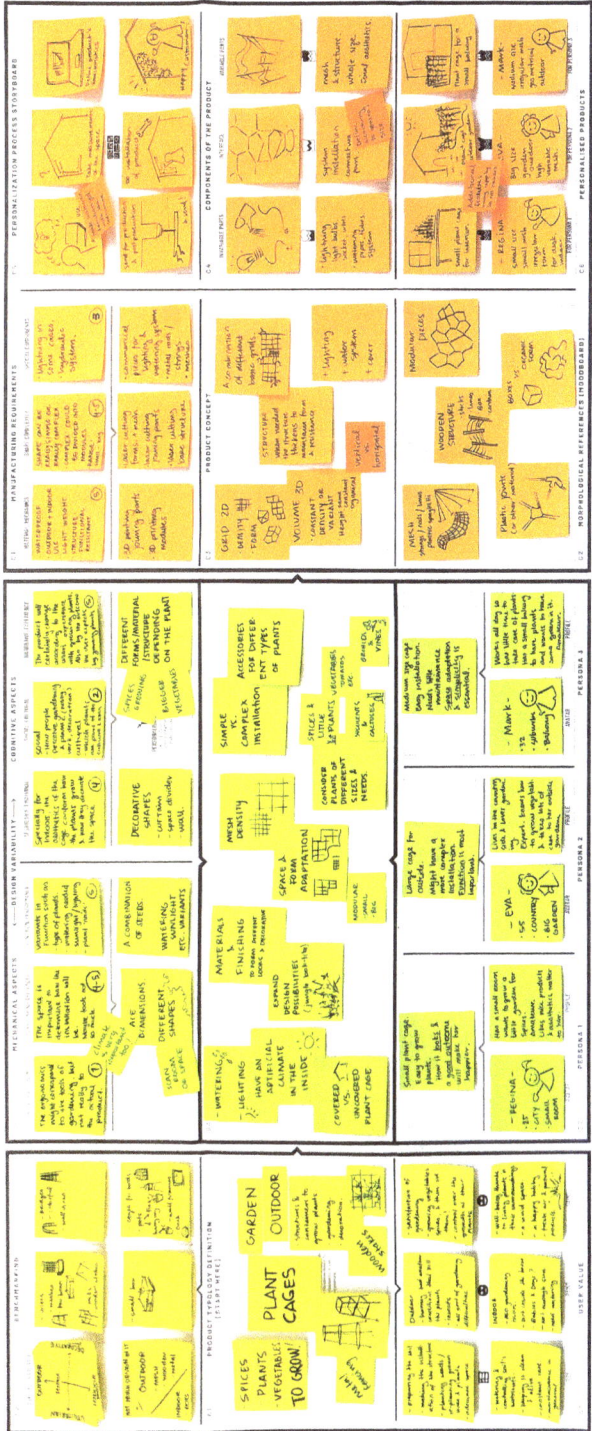

Example of a completed, full size canvas. Differentiating the three main modules also by the post-it colors can facilitate the comprehension. This example was completed in one working day, under supervision from the author, by a test subject already familiar with Computational Design and Digital Fabrication technologies, as well as with personalizable design in general. For design students or professionals with limited prior knowledge of the topic, 2-4 days is a safer estimate for the first attempt of compiling the canvas.

6.6 Design-production-distribution and the Canvas

Designers who work on personalizable products can use a variety of software tools for Computational Design and a variety of hardware tools for Digital Fabrication, depending on the enterprises they work with, the product typology, as well as the aimed users. The business model may vary accordingly, from digital tailormade through the offline use of parametric solid modellers, to an enterprise collaborator who helps to redefine an entire range of products according to the contemporary creative and productive possibilities.

The designer can work also for an extremely lean 'automatized' business model, e.g. a personalization website that relies on an external digital fabrication service bureau. This allows users in the indefinite future to move within the solution space and make orders, to be produced without any significant logistics, thus compensating the designer with a revenue similar to royalties.

The Canvas focuses on the conceptual phase and, as we have seen in chapter 3.6, there are various ways for implementing a Computational Design project. In this section we hint the possibilities of entrepreneurial implementation, outlining how the design-production-distribution process changes, and how would it be possible to connect this renewed process with the inputs and outputs of the Computational Concept Canvas.

Any product design project implies a close relation between design, production and distribution, a process that is coordinated by the actors (client and designer/team) according to their resources, aiming to satisfy the relevant user needs in the best possible way. The 'conventional' design for serial manufacturing is an essentially linear process: clients communicate their requirements to the designer, who researches user needs (maybe together with other professions), then designs a static geometry, that will be reproduced serially, thus constructing a stock of identical products; finally, the sales to individual users can happen through various channels and sometimes many distribution intermediaries.

On the other hand, personalizable design for Digital Fabrication must be a less linear process: even though the design, production and distribution are distinct steps, their outcomes and relations change: the design process leads to a modifiable geometry, fabricated to the specifications of every single user.

The ways of distribution are more direct and must be accurately designed from the first moment, as the personalization interface is integral part of the product concept, as well as the way of delivery. Distribution becomes interactive and experiential by establishing a bi-directional relation: while interacting with the co-design interface, users modify the design project, continuously transmitting their requisites, so there is a real-time feedback loop.

This is a significant difference compared to designing for serial production, where we try to understand user needs as well as possible in the beginning of the design process, then maybe verify the validity of the product before marketing it, but further user feedback in the production phase cannot be integrated (unless in an eventual 'next version' of the product).

The mentioned differences between the conventional and 'updated' design process is illustrated through the scheme of page 96.

Then, page 97 illustrates how Computational Concept Canvas is connected to this 'updated' design process. The input required by the Module A of the Canvas (left) is a product typology on which the designer wants to work; this depends on the topic and interests of the client, e.g. eventual shortages in its product catalogue, or user requisites that cannot be satisfied well enough with serial production. On the other hand, designers can start to work on the canvas seeking to valorise their Computational Design competences, then sell the idea/project to an adequate company or embark on a journey of self-production and start a new firm. In fact, as we have seen, contemporary software tools and fabrication services can allow designers to boot up their own ideas with a minimal investment and extremely lean logistics.

The output side (module C in the right) provides not only (a hypothesis of) the product morphology, but explicitly indicates the manufacturing requirements (C1) and the channel of personalization and distribution (C5). This latter determines the necessary Computational Design tool for designing the modifiable geometry. Therefore, after completing the canvas but before the detailed definition of the product, it's necessary to make some key strategic decisions between available design tools, manufacturing equipment and distribution channels; each of these three choices are mutually determined by the other two. For example, using a complex Computational Design software (low abstraction in our terms: conventional CAD) is more suited to offline personalization, therefore it suggests personalizing and manufacturing directly at the retail venue.

Therefore, if the designer and the client have some limitations regarding the three strategic choices, it is good to keep these in mind while working on the canvas, particularly in the module C. Even though it's not possible to foresee all limitations implied by the concept, it is necessary to define strategically the right combination between the design tool, production venue and channel of distribution.

The scheme on page 97 offers an overview of the main options, further detailed in the next sections.

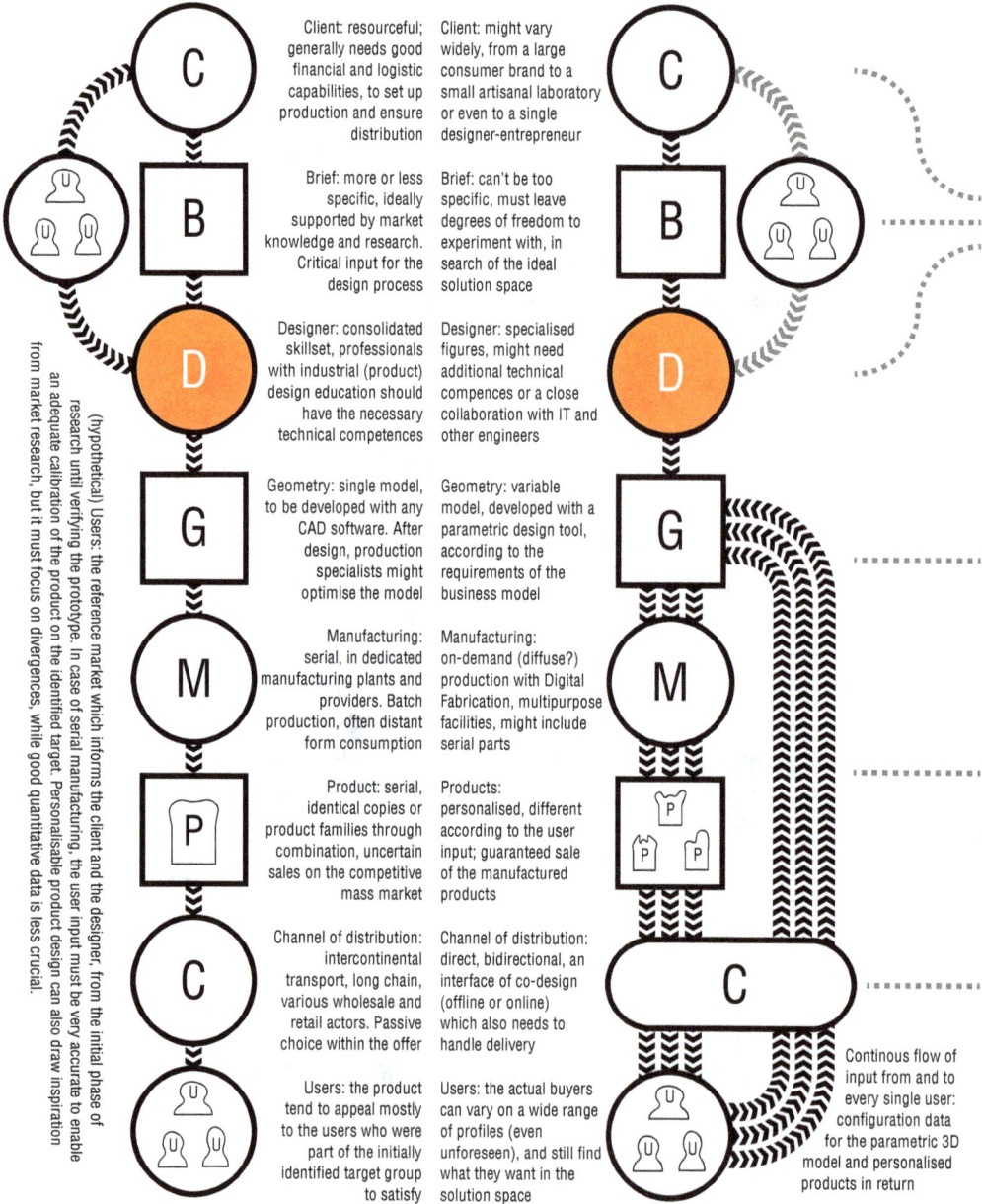

Client: resourceful; generally needs good financial and logistic capabilities, to set up production and ensure distribution

Client: might vary widely, from a large consumer brand to a small artisanal laboratory or even to a single designer-entrepreneur

Brief: more or less specific, ideally supported by market knowledge and research. Critical input for the design process

Brief: can't be too specific, must leave degrees of freedom to experiment with, in search of the ideal solution space

Designer: consolidated skillset, professionals with industrial (product) design education should have the necessary technical competences

Designer: specialised figures, might need additional technical compences or a close collaboration with IT and other engineers

Geometry: single model, to be developed with any CAD software. After design, production specialists might optimise the model

Geometry: variable model, developed with a parametric design tool, according to the requirements of the business model

Manufacturing: serial, in dedicated manufacturing plants and providers. Batch production, often distant form consumption

Manufacturing: on-demand (diffuse?) production with Digital Fabrication, multipurpose facilities, might include serial parts

Product: serial, identical copies or product families through combination, uncertain sales on the competitive mass market

Products: personalised, different according to the user input; guaranteed sale of the manufactured products

Channel of distribution: intercontinental transport, long chain, various wholesale and retail actors. Passive choice within the offer

Channel of distribution: direct, bidirectional, an interface of co-design (offline or online) which also needs to handle delivery

Users: the product tend to appeal mostly to the users who were part of the initially identified target group to satisfy

Users: the actual buyers can vary on a wide range of profiles (even unforeseen), and still find what they want in the solution space

Continous flow of input from and to every single user: configuration data for the parametric 3D model and personalised products in return

(hypothetical) Users: the reference market which informs the client and the designer, from the initial phase of research until verifying the prototype. In case of serial manufacturing, the user input must be very accurate to enable an adequate calibration of the product on the identified target. Personalisable product design can also draw inspiration from market research, but it must focus on divergences, while good quantitative data is less crucial.

COMPUTATIONAL CONCEPT CANVAS

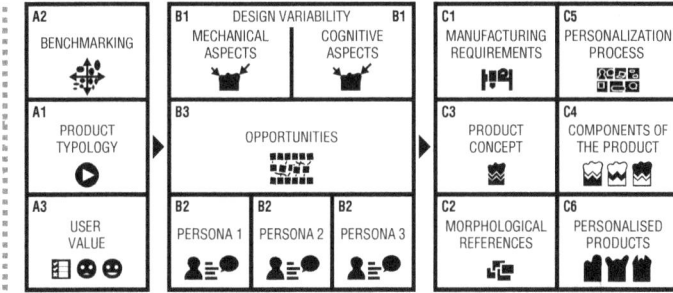

A2 BENCHMARKING	B1 DESIGN VARIABILITY		C1 MANUFACTURING REQUIREMENTS	C5 PERSONALIZATION PROCESS
	B1 MECHANICAL ASPECTS	COGNITIVE ASPECTS		
A1 PRODUCT TYPOLOGY	B3 OPPORTUNITIES		C3 PRODUCT CONCEPT	C4 COMPONENTS OF THE PRODUCT
A3 USER VALUE	B2 PERSONA 1	B2 PERSONA 2 / B2 PERSONA 3	C2 MORPHOLOGICAL REFERENCES	C6 PERSONALISED PRODUCTS

DESIGN

low abstraction: conventional CAD

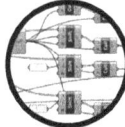

medium abstraction: visual programming

high abstraction: textual programming

PRODUCTION

external digital fabrication provider

directly at the retail point

intervention on the existing factory

DISTRIBUTION

offline: presonal contact

online: web and/or app

mixed: both or a hybrid solution

STRATEGIC CHOICES

Design phase: Computational Design tools

As detailed in chapter 3.6, Computational Design can be practiced using tools that prescribe different levels of abstraction:

- low level of abstraction: 'simple' parametric modelling (e.g. SolidWorks) that promises relatively fast work, but the result is limited morphologically and supposes a business model where personalization is facilitated by a staff that operate as 'digital artisans';
- medium level of abstraction: modelling through visual scripting (e.g. Grasshopper), which requires more specific competences but promises morphologically richer results; personalization can be automatized more substantially and carried out by less specialised staff, also through the web, albeit with limited performance (i.e. not real time, but with delayed visual feedback);
- high level of abstraction: textual programming (e.g. Javascript) which requires a high level of specialisation and/or IT experts in the team, but this approach allows to craft a truly engaging, fluid personalization experience on the web, addressed to a global public.

The product concept resulting from the work on the Canvas often determines the ideal tool; the relevant fields are C4 (variable and invariable components), C5 (personalization process) and C6 (personalized products). Moreover, naturally also the available human resources determine the choice substantially.

Production: Digital Fabrication

Today there are numerous available Digital Fabrication technologies, which operate on different principles, such as 2D cutting from sheets (laser, plasma, waterjet, plotter, router); subtractive 3D manufacturing from blocks (CNC milling or lathe on three or more axis) or additive 3D manufacturing from bulk material (filament, resin, powder). Beyond the exact technology, the most important strategic choice regards the place of production:

- at an external Digital Fabrication service (online or fablabs) it is possible to start production without significant investments, but the times of delivery and the production quality depend on hardly controllable factors;
- at the retail venue with expert (artisan, designer) personnel it is possible to provide a more rapid and flexible service, allowing also a continuous experimentation thanks to the immediate feedback from the users. Offline sales, however, imply an initial investment in the equipment and high operational costs (rent, personnel), if these are not already available to the organisation;
- at the client's factory it is possible to experiment with advanced (also 'dirty') processes, thus optimising production costs, but the necessary investment can be rather high.

Let's note the direct connection to the field C1 (fabrication requirements), which is limited to the discussion of technological requirements; while the field C5 (process) can suggest the ideal place of production.

Distribution: personalization channels

As the previous list of Computational Design tools highlights, there can be two main channels of distribution, which typically serve also as a channel of personalization:

- offline, connected to a physical retail space, which imply a dominantly local market; therefore, the choice can (or must) be guided by expert personnel. In this case, personalization is possible also through a not particularly user-friendly software, eventually offering an amount of choice which would be intimidating without a helping hand. Moreover, a controlled environment allows to gather feedback directly, through observation and verbal interaction;
- online, through the browser or a smartphone application. This allows to access a global market, but it's necessary to provide an effective interface for autonomous personalization. Such efficacy implies the extreme simplification of the choice, the creation of an engaging narrative, or a distant operator who helps to transform user input into an aesthetic and feasible geometry;
- mixed: both online and offline, or a hybrid solution. Any online interface could be used in a retail space as well, but offering different experiences online and offline can help to access a more diverse public, reaching also people who trust less in novelties or virtual shopping.

Beyond the interdependence with the chosen Computational Design tool, the sales channel depends also on the available resources and on the long-term goals of the client or designer. The choice is connected to the C5 field (personalization process) of CCC.

The previous lists highlight the fact that there is no linear path from concept to implementation; one can imagine various starting points, conditions and resources that inform the design journey. Anyways, the schemes on pages 96-97 try to illustrate the possible connections between CCC and the key choices.

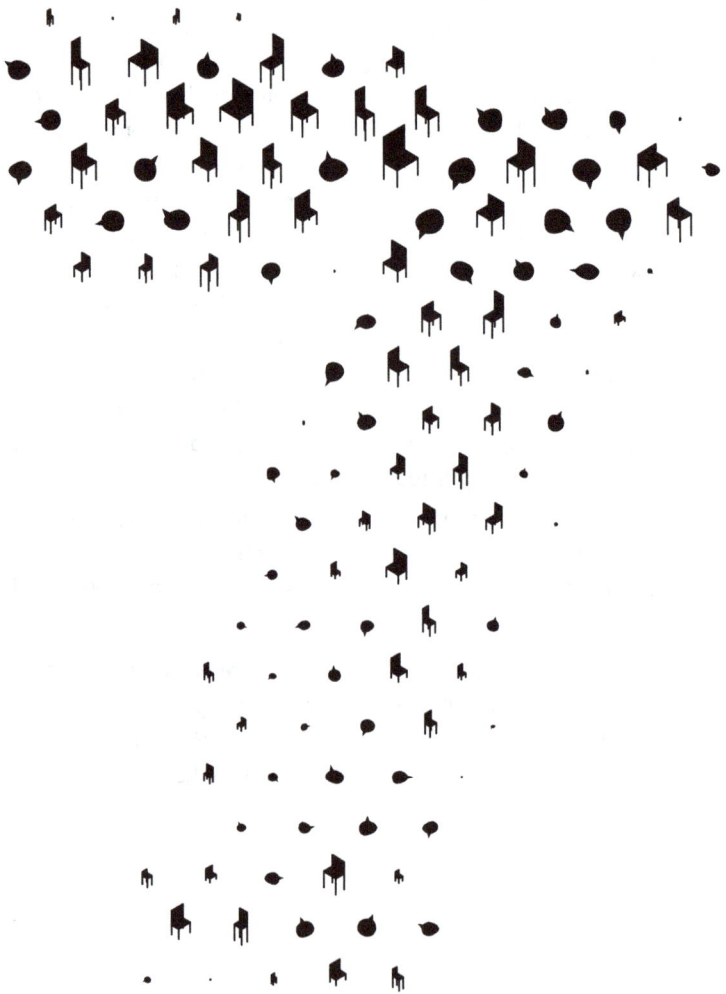

PART III
EVOLUTION
CHAPTER 7
COMPUTATIONAL CONCEPT CANVAS: STEP BY STEP

This chapter is entirely dedicated to the step by step instructions for compiling each of the 3 modules and 12 fields of the Computational Concept Canvas. Please see the previous chapter for the general structure and workflow. Here, each field is coded with a letter-number combination unambiguously recalling the relative fields in each version of the canvas. Each double page contains detailed instructions on the left and an illustration of the given canvas fragment on the right. While the order of description is generally advisable also for the work itself, in many cases the designer might jump backward and forward as new information emerge.

Module A. Product typology definition (left)

A1. Product typology definition [start here]

This is the starting area where the designers enter a product typology to be (computationally) redesigned for Digital Fabrication, aiming for personalization as the key competitive advantage. One should insert the product category name, a brief description, main characteristics, an illustration to explain the general configuration of typical objects in this category, as well as the reason of choice.

The typology should be a well-defined product category which has a market with comparable products. Note that the product typology should be restricted to a reasonable level, at which the available products are easy to confront, and (ideally) a variety of competing products exists, thus indicating the need for personalization. For example, choosing "furniture" as the starting product typology makes further discussion impossibly wide. "Chair" would be a better choice, but it would be even better to restrict the choice to a functional variety which allows the direct confrontation of options, such as "office chair" or "dining room chair". The product typology can come from various sources, e.g. from the product catalogue of the employer/client company, from problems highlighted by market research, from various ideation (brainstorming) techniques, or even from pure intuition to be verified. The canvas was structured as a generic tool to allow work with a wide variety of products, but not all typologies will lead to interesting results. An "unsuccessfully" compiled canvas might indicate that the starting product typology is not an optimal candidate for personalizable products, either because user needs are not divergent enough or because the necessarily invariable elements of the product don't leave enough degrees of freedom for personalization.

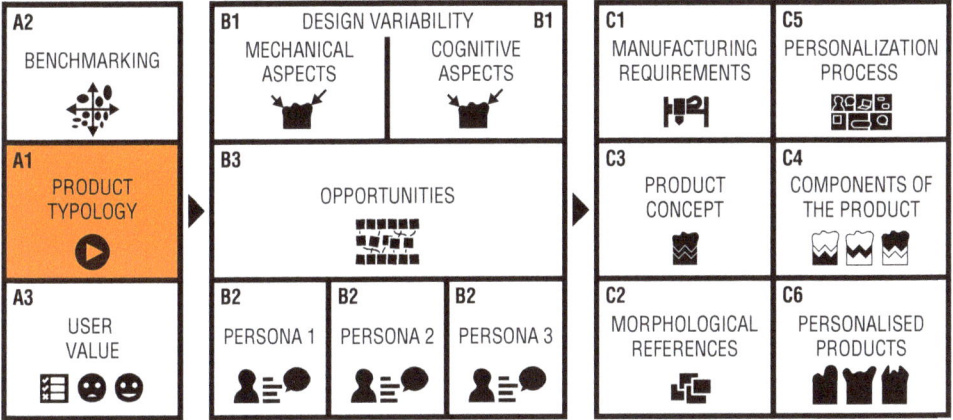

A1

PRODUCT TYPOLOGY DEFINITION
[START HERE]

The starting area where the designers enter the
product typology that they want to redesign for
DF, aiming for a personalisation as a key
competitive advantage.

A2. Benchmarking

Exploration of the current variety within the chosen product typology, through a set of examples (photos or drawings) organized according to the observable tendencies. The field should describe also the criteria of evaluation. The benchmarking should highlight how much divergence is there among currently existing products in the category, hence indicating if there is already a need for personalization. Designers should focus on divergences in usage, ergonomics or design language, rather than technical performance, quality or price.

The large-scale (post-it) versions of the canvas offer space for benchmarking on a "cartesian" (x-y axis) graph, which asks for defining two important dimensions, each with two opposite extreme values. Mapping products according to these axes might reveal currently uncovered areas.

The compact versions (A4/A3 format) of the canvas don't have the space necessary for the cartesian mapping of images/drawings, therefore these call for inserting a written synthesis of the observable tendencies within the product typology.

Regardless the canvas format, the cartesian mapping might not work well for certain products, so it might be disregarded in favour of a more adequate logic of classification.

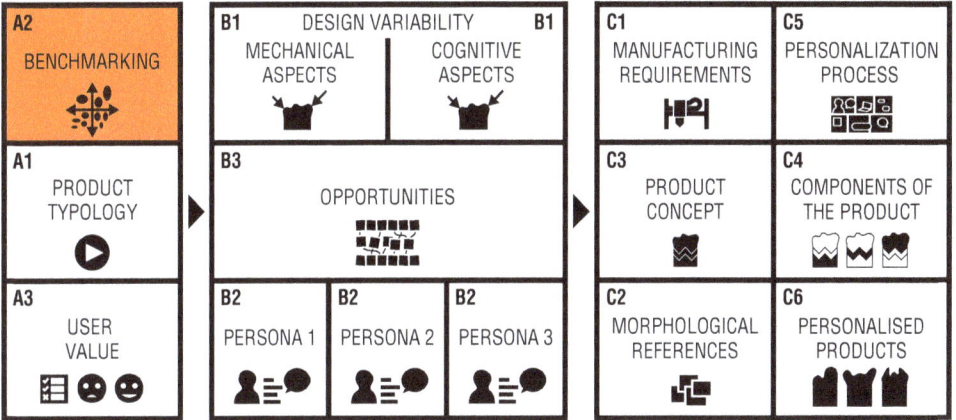

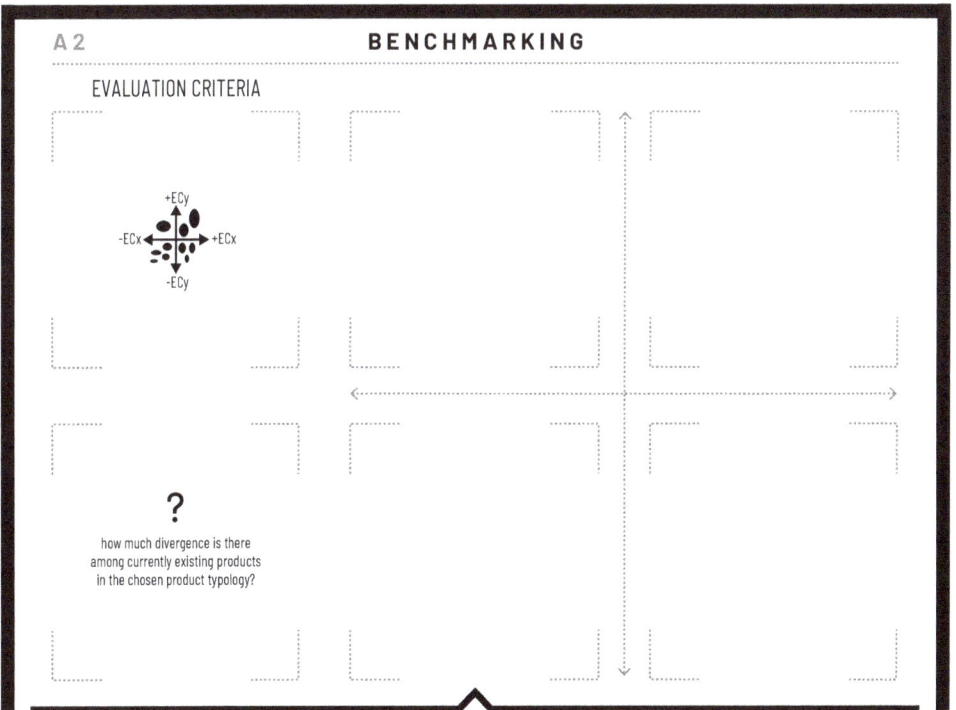

A3. User value

The third square in the bottom with the title "Usage" helps to clarify the product typology's *raison d'être* by analysing the jobs users want to carry out with the product, the pains (difficulties) they might experience during the usage and the gains they hope to obtain as a result. This analysis should help the designer to clarify and record the basic expectations as well as the advanced aspirations regarding the product typology.

In this field, designers should try to list as many elements as possible, considering a variety of different user profiles. Later on, the adjacent "Personas" fields will give space for a more detailed and specific analysis of user needs and desires. In fact, the later work with the personas might motivate an update to the list of jobs, pains and gains.

These aspects have been derived from the Value Proposition Canvas (connected to the Business Model Canvas) described by Osterwalder (2014). However, in this case we are not yet assessing a precise value proposition (which will be the final result of our canvas), nor do we have a precise customer profile: on the contrary, the point of the personalizable design is to appeal to a variety of different user groups. Therefore, the goal of this field is to create an overview of all the potential customer jobs, pains and gains related to the given product category. Osterwalder (2014, p. 10-17) offers comprehensive descriptions and suggestions; synthetic descriptions are cited below:

Jobs describe the things your customers are trying to get done in their work or in their lives. A customer job could be the tasks they are trying to perform and complete, the problems they are trying to solve, or the needs they are trying to satisfy. https://assets.strategyzer.com/assets/resources/customer-jobs-trigger-questions.pdf

Pains describe anything that annoys your customers before, during, and after trying to get a job done or simply prevents them from getting a job done. Pains also describe risks, that is, potential bad outcomes, related to getting a job done badly or not at all. https://assets.strategyzer.com/assets/resources/customer-pains-trigger-questions.pdf

Gains describe the outcomes and benefits your customers want. Some gains are required, expected, or desired by customers, and some would surprise them. Gains include functional utility, social gains, positive emotions, and cost savings. More info at https://assets.strategyzer.com/assets/resources/customer-gains-trigger-questions.pdf

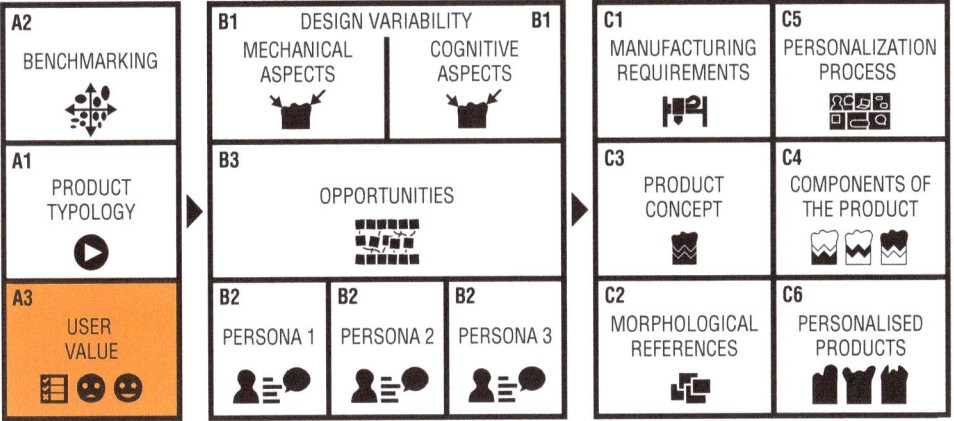

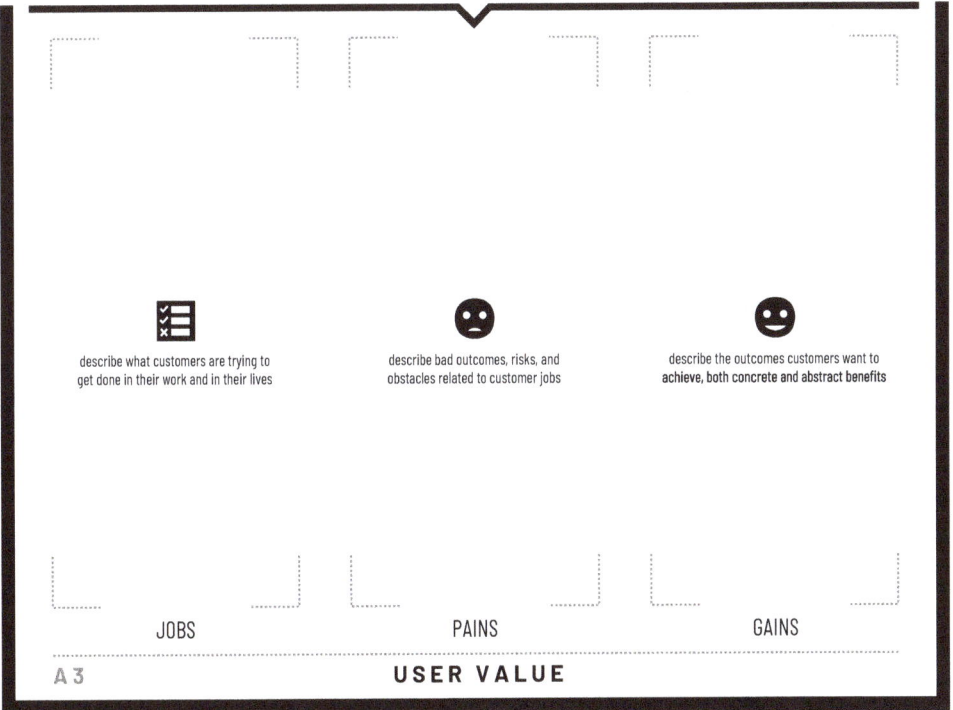

describe what customers are trying to get done in their work and in their lives

describe bad outcomes, risks, and obstacles related to customer jobs

describe the outcomes customers want to achieve, both concrete and abstract benefits

JOBS   PAINS   GAINS

A 3   **U S E R   V A L U E**

Module B. Personalization principle definition (center)

B1.1 Design Variability

Area of key importance, where the designer analyzes how much the previously mentioned 6 variable aspects (derived from case studies) determine the shape, usage and perceived value of the product. Each of these aspects are evaluated on a 1 to 5 scale according to a specific question, and the motivations are registered on a post-it note.

Mechanical aspects:

- Physiology/Ergonomics: How much do physiological variations among users determine the design, usage or perceived value of the product?
- Environment/Objects: How much do other objects and the environment determine the design, usage or perceived value of the product?
- Function/Performance: How much do extra functions and performance determine the design, usage or perceived value of the product?

Cognitive aspects:

- Aesthetic/Emotional: How much do personal aesthetic taste and emotional response determine the design, usage or perceived value of the product?
- Social/Cultural: How much do the social-cultural belonging of the targeted user determine the design, usage or perceived value of the product?
- Narrative/Experience: How much do a narrative or the user's experience determine the design, usage or perceived value of the product?

This field relies on the capacity of the designer to critically assess the design of existing products, building on the observations in the previously completed fields of the canvas (A2. Benchmarking and A3. User value). As a starting point of the evaluation, products on the market should be considered as reference. If there is a lot of variety among them, it should be relatively easy to identify the dominant aspects along which the offer diverges. However, variable user needs are not always manifested in products on the market, so the questions should be approached freely and creatively, especially regarding the cognitive aspects. Artisanal/tailor-made production, functional or aesthetic accessories, post-market modifications or decorations might indicate an existing (even if marginal) need for more variation within the product typology, not addressed by the current serial production. Hence, even if on the current market a product's design vary only slightly, the perceived value and usage of that design might vary significantly, which can justify the development of personalizable products.

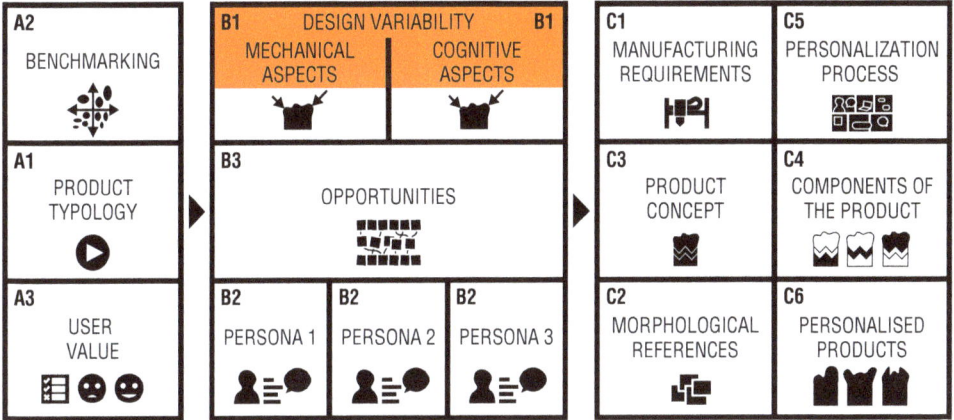

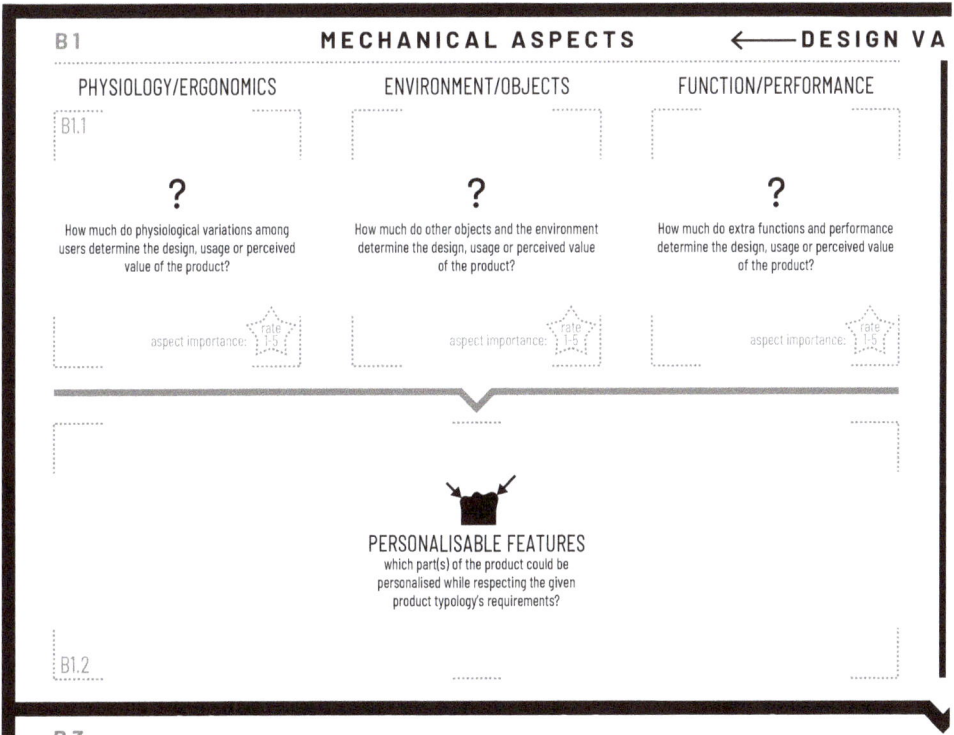

B1.2 Personalizable features

Here the designer should reflect on how the most interesting variable aspects (evaluated in B1.1) might influence the design of the features of the product, respecting the given typology's functional requirements. This field should clarify which part(s) of the product can be personalized, while respecting the basic functional requirements of the given product typology.

According to the previous evaluation on the 1 to 5 star scale, the most interesting aspect(s) should be considered, while ignoring those with low ratings. This might result that one of the two B1.2 fields remain empty, which is normal, and it would indicate that the given product typology is not adequate for personalization according to mechanical or cognitive aspects.

If, however, all star ratings remain low, it might indicate that the product typology is not adequate for personalization at all. In this case, it is still possible to proceed anyways with constructing personas in the B2, which might help new ideas to emerge regarding the variable aspects. Otherwise, the designer should refine the choice of product typology.

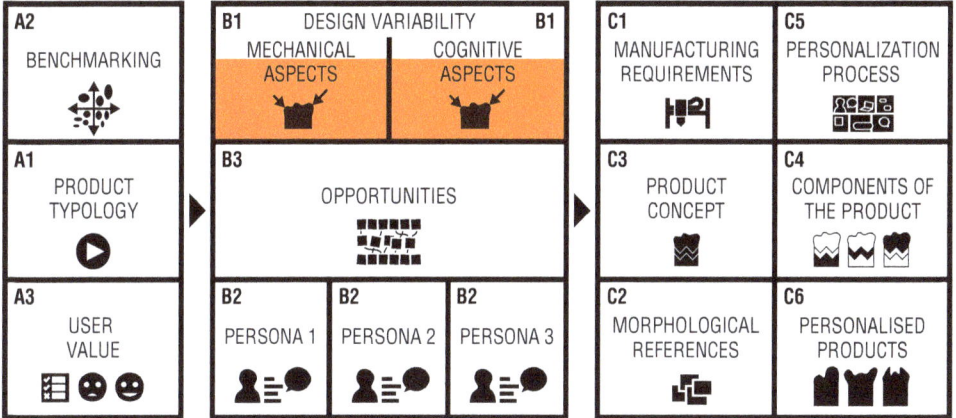

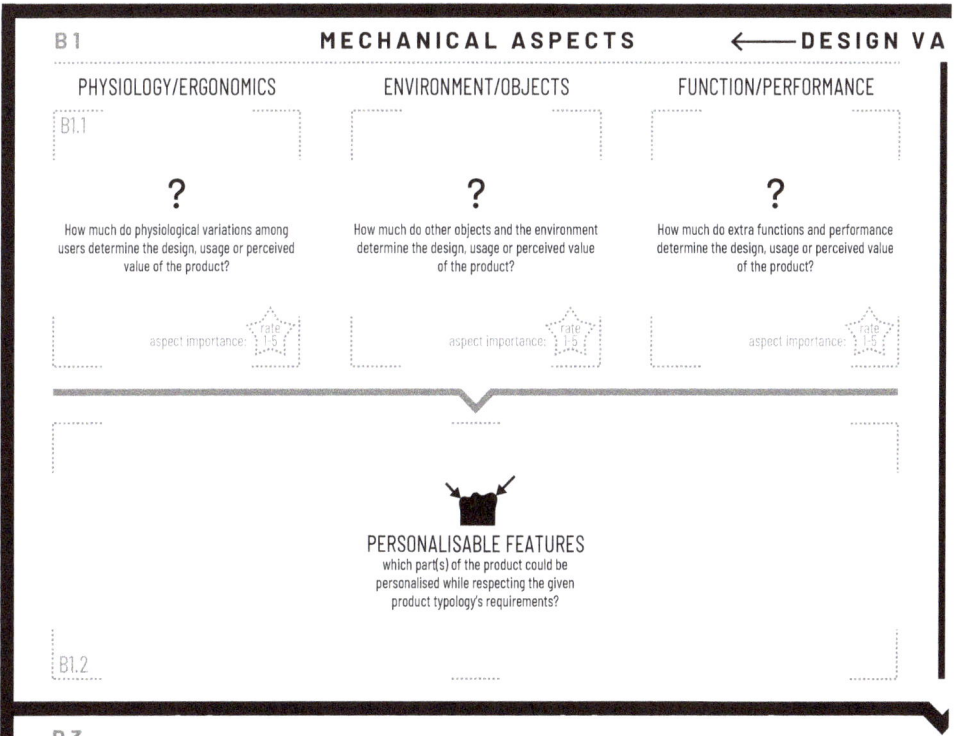

B2.1 Profile and avatar

In order to comprehend whether user needs are sufficiently divergent to justify a personalizable product, in this area the designer constructs three 'imaginary' user profiles according to the widespread *personas* technique. According to the best practices, ideally the personas are synthetized from data collected from interviews and other sources, in order to capture the environment, goals, skills, attitudes and behaviour of hypothesised groups of users. To create empathy and allow quantitative work, fictional personal details and an evocative avatar (drawing or photo) are added, making the *persona* a realistic character for whom to design.

Since the work on the Computational Concept Canvas is focused on personalizable design, the constructed *personas* should have markedly different expectations from the chosen product typology.

The three constructed *personas* will help not only in the following phase of ideation, but also in the final verification of the concept in the C6 field, where the designer should imagine how the three imagined users might want to personalize their products.

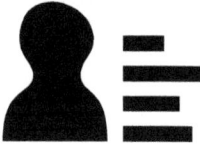

B2.2 Personalization need

After constructing the *personas*, in these fields the designer should insert ideas regarding their most particular needs, which would motivate them to engage in a personalization process.

Note that the *personas* field is positioned nearby the User value field of the first module (A3): the variety of possible jobs, pains and gains registered there should be reflected also in *personas* profiles and their needs. On the other hand, newly emerged elements in B2 might help to go back and update the A3 field.

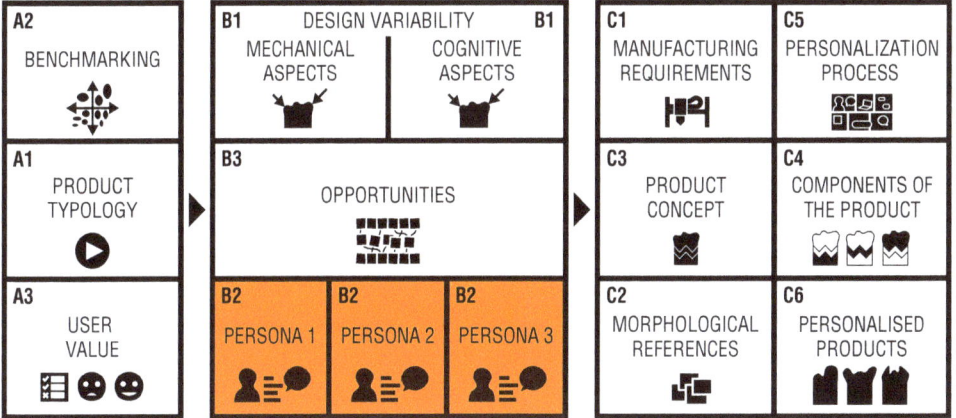

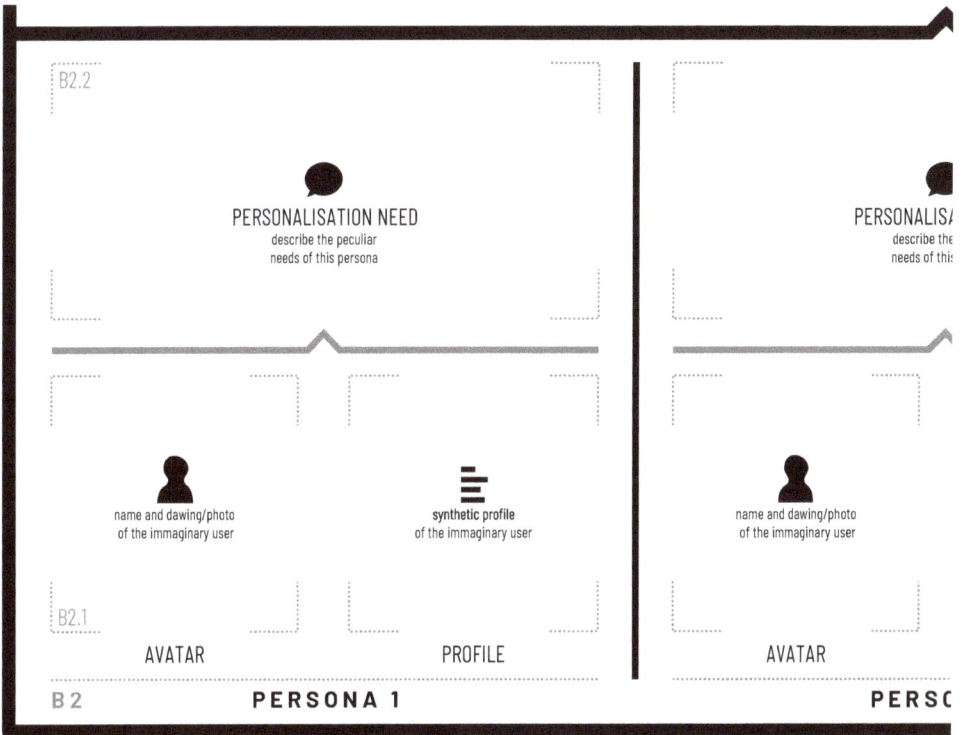

B3. Opportunities

In this area, the designer should connect the possibly personalizable features (B1.2) with the identified personalization needs (B2.2).

The ample and unstructured space is open for idea generation, allowing to dedicate the necessary number of post-its to ideas, ideally connected to previous observations; connections should be marked e.g. with sticky paper tape. The designer should try to identify which personalizable features have the strongest connections to the identified personalization needs, resulting in more defined ideas about the desirable configuration and morphology of the final product. However, in this phase it is not yet necessary to define precisely the product concept, it is more important to map out many opportunities and focus on connections.

If a personalization need (and the relative design variability aspect) is strongly connected to every personas' needs, it is a good indicator that the product should be personalizable for that aspect. However, ideas of personalization might come up even regardless the previously analyzed three personas, which can't represent accurately all the possible users.

On the other hand, personas might give ideas for previously not revealed personalizable features; the designer should handle B3 as an area for a brainstorming that can far away from the starting ideas. Nonetheless, previous analytical steps are important in order to create a solid understanding of the product typology and its potential users before the brainstorming.

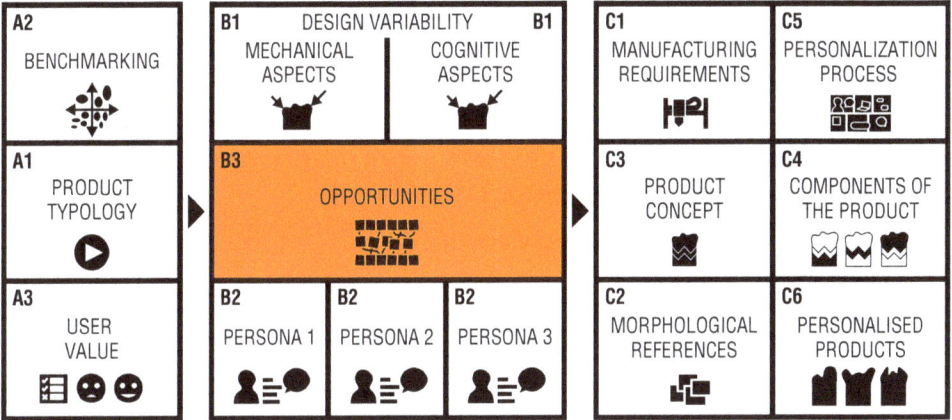

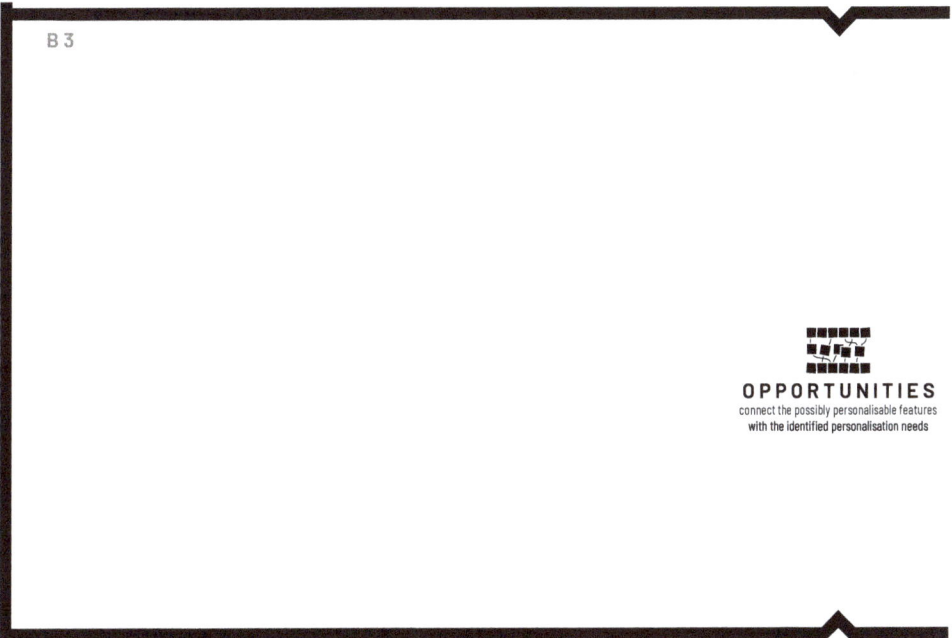

OPPORTUNITIES

connect the possibly personalisable features
with the identified personalisation needs

Module C. Detailed concept definition (right)

C1.1 Manufacturing requirements

Approaching the final concept, the designer analyzes the requirements that determine the feasibility of the previously identified product/feature opportunities, trying to find the ideal Digital Fabrication technology.

For the ease of discussion, the manufacturing requirements are divided according to three aspects:

- Material/Mechanics requirements: what are the most demanding mechanical forces and material requirements for the product?
- Shape/Structure complexity: what kind of morphological and dimensional constraints must the product satisfy?
- Special Components: what (if any) special components are necessary for the product to work properly?

Similarly to the nearby B1.1 fields, beyond the verbal assessment the feasibility of these aspects should be rated on a 1 to 5 scale, where lower ratings indicate harder to satisfy requirements, to which extra attention must be paid.

Apart from the achievable shapes, the choice of production technology can heavily influence also the achievable price point, consumer relations and business model in general. Therefore, this field should be considered an important step of design strategy definition.

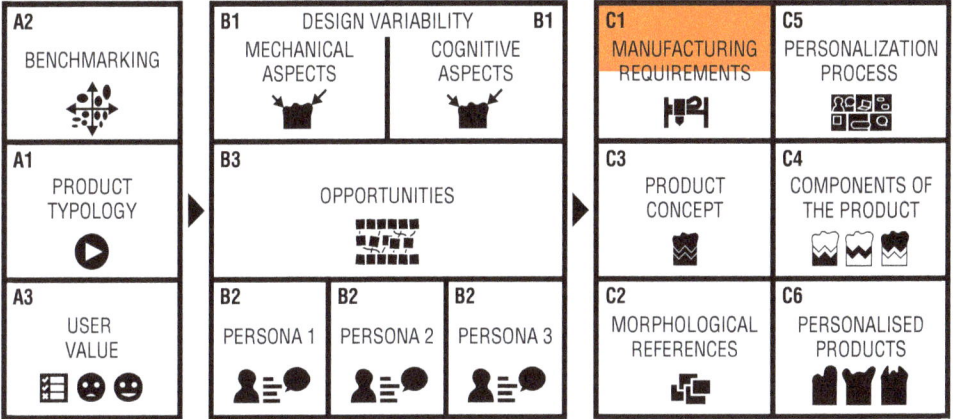

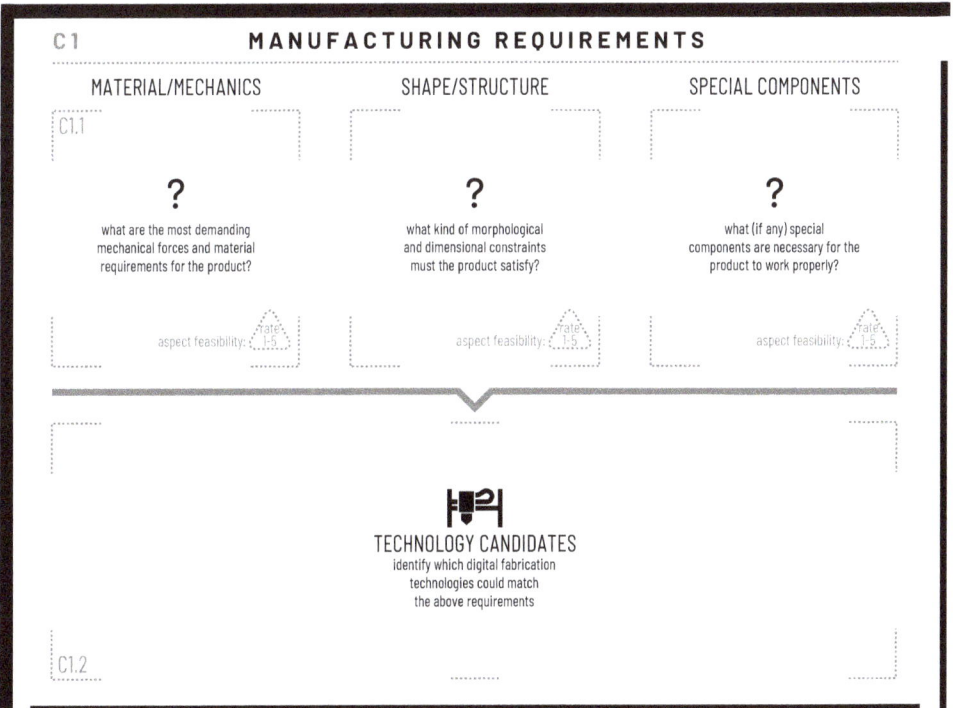

C1.2 Technology candidates

In this field, the designer should identify which digital fabrication technologies could match the above requirements. This step supposes the knowledge of at least the fundamental characteristics of the main digital fabrication technologies operating with different principles, such as 2d cutting planar surfaces (laser, plasma, waterjet, CNC router, CNC plotter) 3d milling blocks of material (CNC mill with 3 or more axis, CNC lathe) or 3d printing (from filament, resin, powder). An expert knowledge and hands-on access to these technologies is welcome but not indispensable, since today various online service offers comprehensive information and immediate price estimates regarding many mainstream digital fabrication technologies.

Beyond the digitally manufactured components, the product might include parts which must be realized with conventional, serial manufacturing technologies; these parts and technologies (materials) should be listed as well. The chosen manufacturing option will determine also the logistics, timeframe and costs of the production, as well as the reasonable way of personalization and in general the business model. Therefore, the C1.2 field will help to articulate better the final concept, or to turn back in the ideation phase or even re-evaluate the validity of the starting product category. The contents of the C1 field are not necessarily easy to compile without a more precise morphological hypothesis; therefore, it might be necessary to review the assessment when the next fields (especially C3 and C4) are done. While initially it is a good idea to list multiple options, the final version of the canvas should have the also the final choice clarified in the C1.2 field. As a reminder, let's overview the (constantly evolving) range of digital fabrication options:

2D cutting from flat sheets. Technology: laser, waterjet, CNC router, CNC plotter. Materials: very wide range, with various limitation.
3D milling from block. Technology: 3 or more axes milling machine, cnc lathe. Materials: solid, but not too much (complicates processing).
3D printing from filament. Technology: FDM: various economical and expensive machines. Materials: wide range of plastic, clay, hybrid filaments.
3D printing with powder. Technology: SLS: sintering or laser melting, direct to indirect thanks to binder. Materials: typically plastic, ceramic, sandstone, metal; variable costs and limitations.
Liquid resin 3D printing. Technology: stereolithography or resin casting. Materials: special hardenable photo resins, different mechanical properties and colors.
Hybrid technologies, e.g. cutter + thermoforming, stereolithography + lost wax, wire print + silicone casting

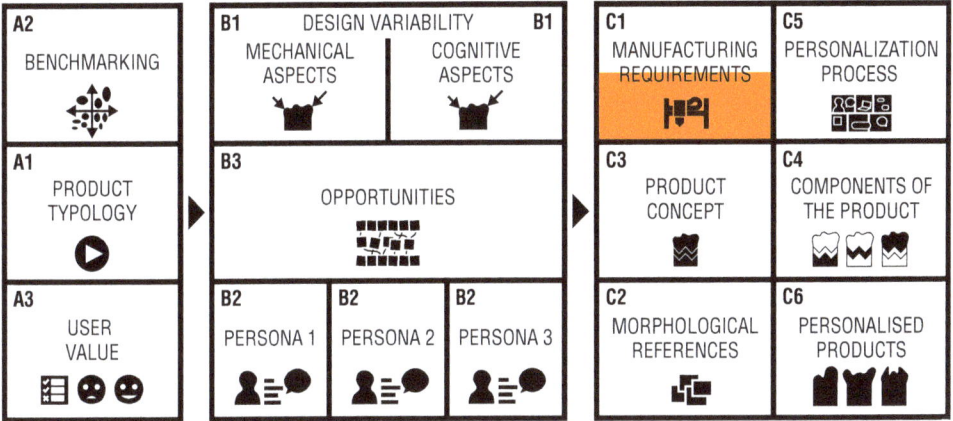

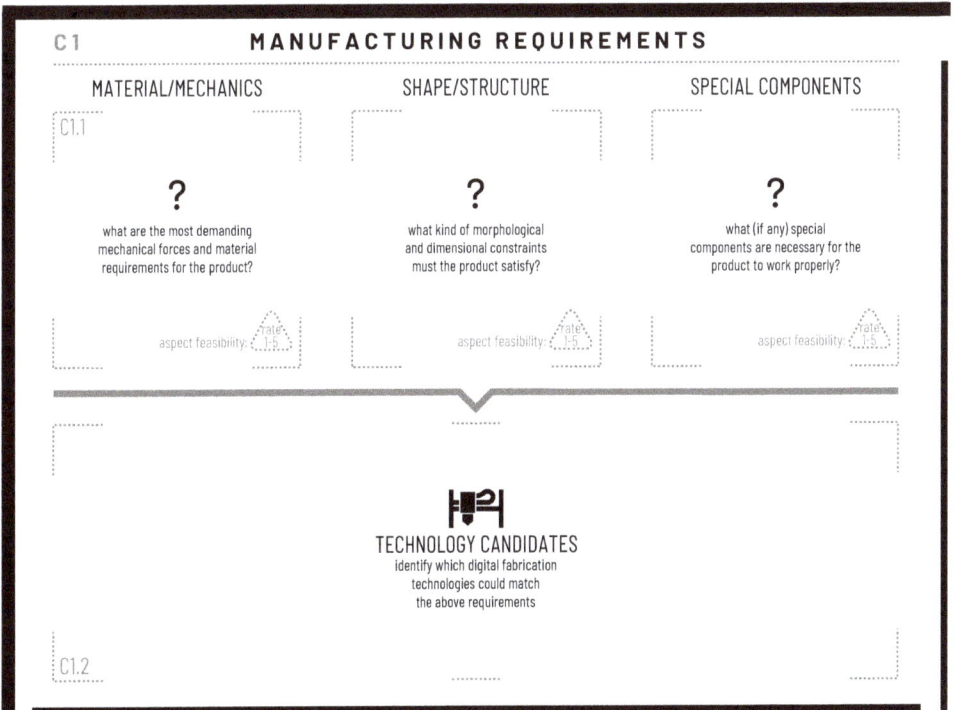

C2. Morphological references (moodboard)

This field illustrates the expected visual qualities of the final object through a collection of images and/or text description. The morphological references (moodboard) should be coherent with the range of previously constructed personas (see the neighbouring B2 fields).

Even though the goal of the Computational Concept Canvas is to obtain a variable design which is dependent on a significant (or even creative) user input, the designer still has to define the range of possibilities (solution space) and the design language from where the personalization process starts. When mechanical aspects are prevalent for the personalization, then the starting design language will dominate the aesthetic value of the object. If, however, there is a strong cognitive component in the personalization, then the (creative) contribution of the user can have a major importance in defining the aesthetic appeal of the product.

According to the personalizable aspects, the visual references gathered in this field should help to shape the invariable parts of the design and to hypothesize a reliable way of transforming the user input into high quality design. If strong brand identity is a goal, even a significant and creative user input can be transformed into recognizable design, but it needs a conscious effort of defining the aimed visual qualities.

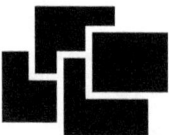

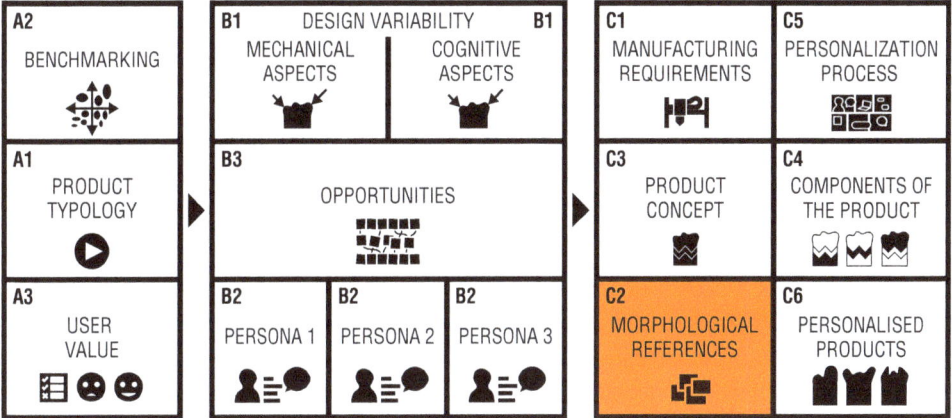

illustrate the expected visual qualities
of the final object through a collection
of images and/or text description

C2   **MORPHOLOGICAL REFERENCES (MOODBOARD)**

C3. Product concept

This field contains the morphological concept of the product, considering an 'average' personalization. Based on the previous analytical work and ideation, the overall design should be illustrated, as detailed and precise as possible, providing a preview of the final product. The ideas gathered in the neighbouring B3 field are synthetized (by selecting and/or combining the best ones) and passed through the feasibility filter of the C1 field and aesthetic vision defined in the C2 field.

As mentioned earlier, the product's shape and the production technology strongly influence each other, so after this field it might be necessary to update the previous C1. This concept sketch should be sufficient to start creating a CAD model of the product, therefore it is necessary to arrive to a level of detail which illustrates not only the general composition of the volumes, but also the connection between the surfaces. Therefore, more than one view might be necessary, but there is no need to make 'correct' technical drawings with dimensions etc.

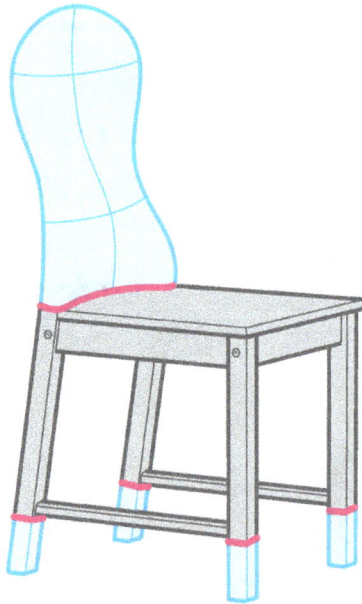

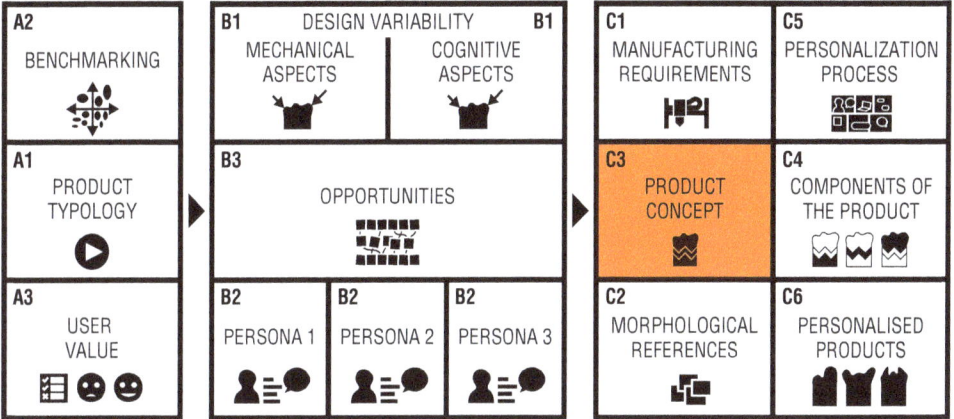

A2 BENCHMARKING	B1 DESIGN VARIABILITY		C1 MANUFACTURING REQUIREMENTS	C5 PERSONALIZATION PROCESS

C3   PRODUCT CONCEPT

morphological concept of the product
considering an 'average' personalisation

C4. Components of the product

Further illustrating the concept outlined in the C3 field, here the designer should distinguish between the variable and invariable parts of the design, highlighting also where they meet.

Variable parts are those which can be personalized through parametric design, to be manufactured with digital fabrication.

Invariable parts are those which cannot be personalized, either because they need to have a given geometry in order to function properly, or because personalization would not change the object's perceived value. Invariable parts can be produced by either digital fabrication or conventional serial production; this latter can be necessary for obtaining certain material performances (e.g. special mechanical properties, chemical or heat resistance) or for allowing advanced functionalities (e.g. electronics). If a part is obtainable both through digital and conventional manufacturing, it is worth considering whether the business model allow the higher upfront investment and logistical burden of the serial production, or it is more advantageous to keep the production flexible even if it implies higher cost per part.

Finally, under 'interface' the designer should describe the critical surface where variable and invariable parts meet. Connecting two solid volumes, the interface is a surface, however it can be represented by a line, as the connecting surface itself is invisible – at least on the complete, mounted product. Note that the distinction between variable and invariable parts is a logical rather than physical difference: a single physical component (made by digital fabrication) can have both variable and invariable parts. Nonetheless, they should be distinguished in order to facilitate the later phase of parametric modelling.

In order to help understanding and communication, it is recommended to distinguish the three kinds of components by color-coding, e.g. grey: invariables, cyan: variables, magenta: interface. In case of a compact version canvas, the work can be limited to text notes.

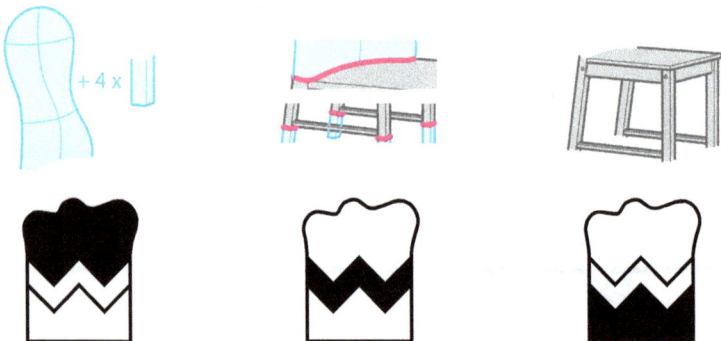

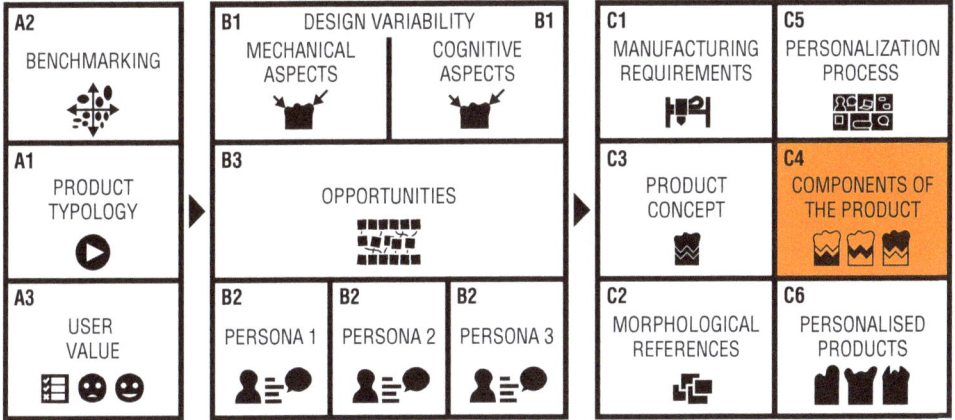

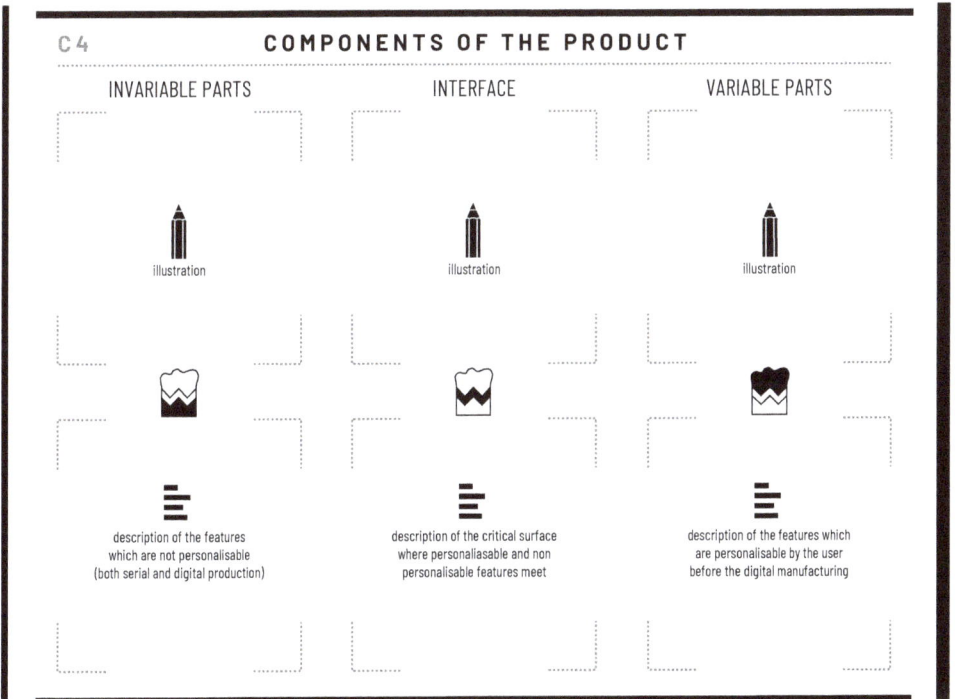

C5. Personalization Process Storyboard

This field contains an illustration and description of the main steps necessary to obtain the custom product.

Mapping the customer (or user) journey is already a widespread practice in design, and this technique can take many different shapes according to the nature of the product/service, as well as the graphic skills of the designer. As far as the Computational Concept Canvas Concerned, a storyboard is recommended, with rich text notes.

Based on one of the previously constructed *personas,* the storyboard should begin with the emergence of the personalization need and proceed with the *persona* entering in interaction with the system of personalization, either online in the browser and smartphone apps, or offline in a physical shop.

The main input of the user should be illustrated, as well as any important actions necessary from the staff of the selling company. Finally, the storyboard should indicate the way and timeframe of delivery and any eventual post-purchase interaction between user and company, e.g. the integration with additional digital services that may enhance the value of the product.

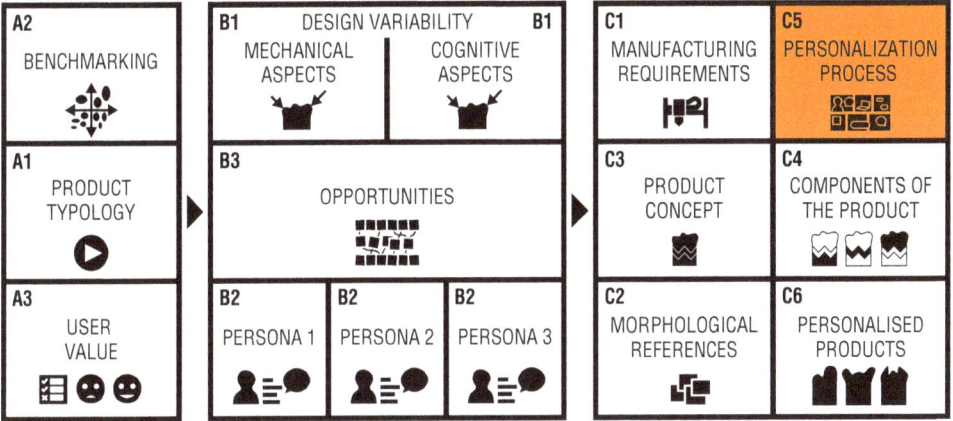

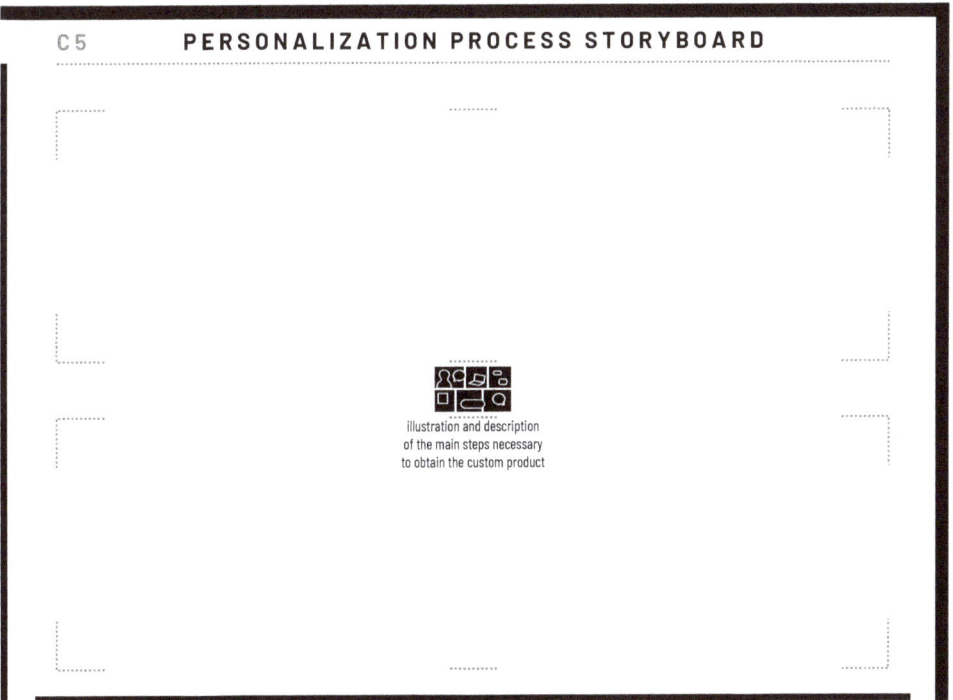

C6. Personalized Products

This field should illustrate and describe briefly three hypotheses of the product, personalized for the three previously constructed personas (B2).

If the personalization process includes a creative contribution of the user (not only a simple measurement or anatomical scanning), the notable differences in the creative input should be described and/or illustrated as well.

This field serves as a thought experiment of the elaborated concept: if the product idea is valid and the personas are well constructed, then the resulting three drawings should be markedly different and highlight why personalization creates an otherwise unobtainable value for the user. Moreover, these drawings can help to start 3d modelling realistic previews of the product, as well as to structure adequately the parametric model, keeping in mind the potential difficulties.

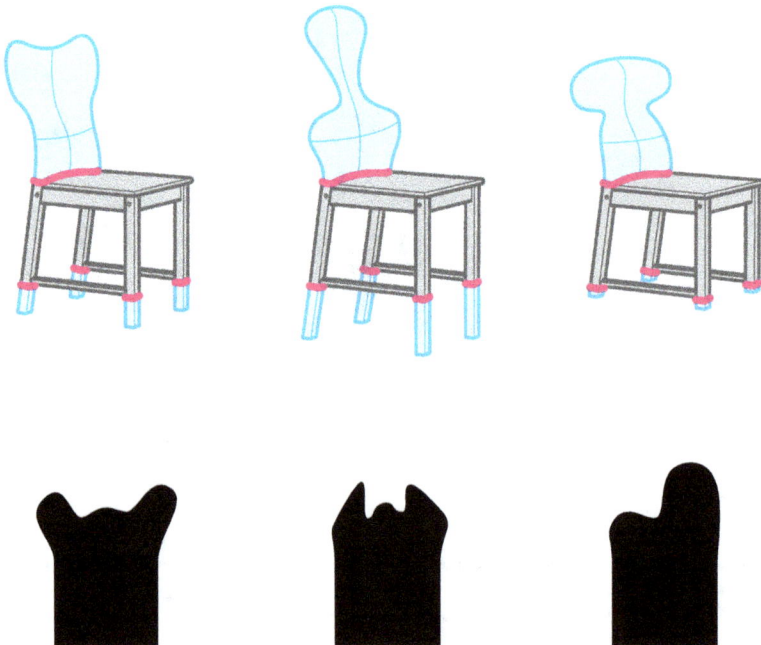

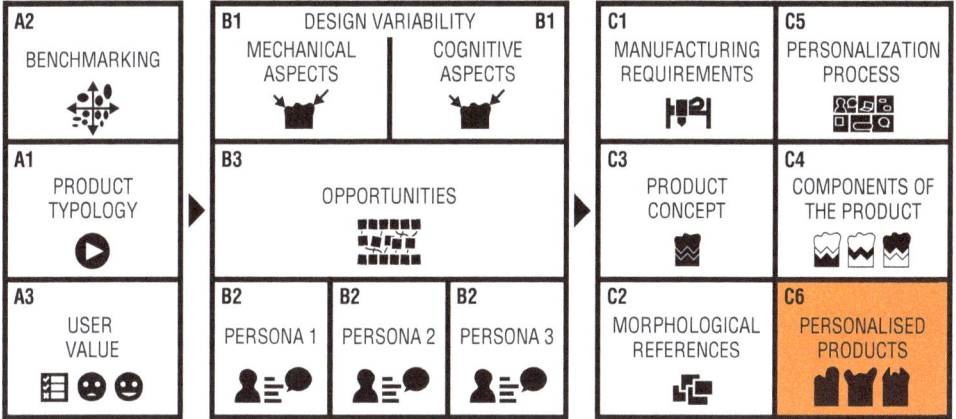

hypothesise how persona 1 would personalise the product, including eventual differences in user input

hypothesise how persona 2 would personalise the product, including eventual differences in user input

hypothesise how persona 3 would personalise the product, including eventual differences in user input

FOR PERSONA 1   FOR PERSONA 2   FOR PERSONA 3

C6   **P E R S O N A L I S E D   P R O D U C T S**

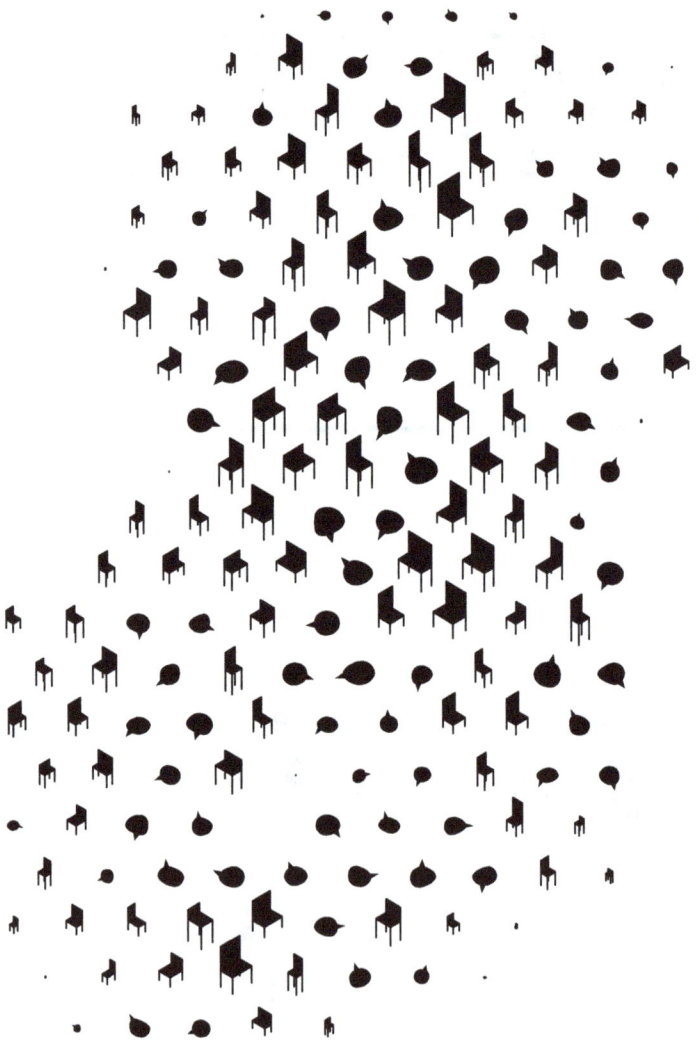

EVOLUTION / TRAINING

PART III
EVOLUTION
CHAPTER 8
TRAINING FOR PERSONALIZABLE PRODUCT DESIGN

The previous chapters presented a new design workflow and the relative design tool. These were born out of the necessity of teaching personalizable (Computational) Design for Digital Fabrication to Product Design students, motivating them to reflect deeply on how user needs may diverge, in order to make them consider a wide range of personalization options. Moreover, as these teaching activities were parallel to a long-standing research activity of a fabrication lab, we were (and still are) curious also about how much space there is for personalizable design in the everyday environment, so we aimed to demonstrate whether and how personalizable design could be desirable in a wide variety of contexts and product typologies. This chapter will illustrate a series of didactic activities focused on personalizable design, both using the Computational Concept Canvas with the related workflow and using other approaches. The described situations range from a few days long workshop to an entire semester of teaching.

Overview – teaching "digital native" product design

Experimenting personal fabrication with university students is not new: for example, MIT's recurring course "How to make almost anything" since 2001 demonstrates how empowering Digital Fabrication can be for creating unique objects (Gershenfeld, 2005). Another, more recent example is the Berlin-based teaching/research project "Beyond Prototyping" (Ängeslevä et al., 2016). This project was focused on designing feasible products that are easily personalizable through online services, yet offering the aesthetic quality that one would expect in design-oriented retail, rather than technological demos; after the teaching experience, some projects were further developed and made available for purchase.

Even considering the many related examples, there seems to be no strong attempt to guide and visualise the conceptual design process of personalizable products, nonetheless the apparent difficulty; this was part of the motivation for developing the Computational Concept Canvas. This development relied on teaching experiences with product design students, who helped to test the first version of the canvas; the CCC described in the previous chapter is, actually, the revised final version.

This chapter will illustrate a series of didactic activities oriented to personalizable design, partially using the Computational Concept Canvas:

- •8.1 exploring personalizbility across many product typologies, based on randomly selected keywords. One semester course titled "Post-Series Design" for third year BSc students of industrial design. This course was an ideal testbed for Computationl Concepts Canvas which was used mainly in an initial three-week ideation workshop, after which it was expanded slowly.
- •8.2 exploring personalizability in a specific product typology: international workshop "Design your Roman Holiday", with the theme of personalizable souvenirs. As time was limited, rather than filling a predefined tool (canvas), in this case we did more freeform conversations and analysis, partially on the streets of the city.
- •8.3 mapping the progress: inserting the above mentioned and other (thesis) projects into the framework of six variabilities, described in chapter 4. Evaluating the new projects with the usual radar diagrams illustrates how the world of personalizable design can be extended in many directions.

8.1 Post-Series Design. One semester course.

As mentioned, the proposed method of concept development through a canvas tool was experimented with a class of industrial design students. This section describes the experience of the one-semester product design atelier course, held for third year Bachelor students of Industrial (product) Design at Sapienza University of Rome.[1]

---

[1] The author collaborated on the course with the course responsible Prof. Loredana Di Lucchio and tutors Alex Coppola and Ainee Alamo Avila. Prototyping carried out in collaboration with Marco Chialastri and Sapienza Design Factory.

The course titled "Post Series Design" aims to prepare the students for a cultural-productive environment where the market is extremely segmented and has various alternatives in every product category of significant economic interest. In order to promote competitivity in such environment, the course focuses on the idea of personalizability as distinctive value, through Computational Design and Digital Fabrication. Beyond the educational objectives, the course had the research objective of verifying the Computational Concept Canvas tool, which was slightly improved according to the course's feedback.

In order to stimulate the exploration of a wide range of products, there was no specific topic assigned, but the 20 working groups have extracted six keywords derived from the exhibition "Neo Preistoria: 100 Verbi", held at La Triennale of Milan in 2016, curated by Andrea Branzi (Branzi and Hara, 2016). This exhibition revolved around 100 key actions representative of modern life and thus modern industrial production; starting ideation from these gave the opportunity to re-evaluate these actions with in the contemporary industrial scenario of spreading Digital Fabrication. Therefore, the class of 55 was divided in six macro-groups of 3-4 groups, each of which had 2-3 students.

As a first step, each student was asked to bring one object that could help carrying out the action associated to their own macro-group. These objects helped to ignite a discussion on the meaning of the keyword (action), different objects that could help carrying out such actions, their circumstances, the 'relatives' of the chosen objects; finally, each group have identified a product typology to work on for the rest of the semester; students were encouraged to choose an object typology which stimulated a lot of divergent or even contradicting opinions/expectations; this should indicate better personalization potential.

Analysis and ideation workshop – CCC Canvas

The described problem finding workshop helped to provide the necessary input for the next workshop based on the Computational Concept Canvas. Since the previous chapters already described the workflow in detail, this section is limited to discussing the actual experience of working with the tool. Each of the 20 groups had a canvas to work on during the tree operative days of the workshop, divided approximately in the following way:

- day 1: analysis of the product category through examples, the jobs-pains-gains framework (left column) and the system of variabilities derived from the case studies (top-centre row);
- day 2: construction of personas and analysis of their needs, connecting them to the possibility of variation, i.e. feature ideation (bottom row, central field);
- day 3: establishment of the product concept and user journey through a storyboard, presentation of findings in front of the entire class (right column).

As usual in the design atelier courses, the abilities of the students have determined the pace of the process, and so did the product category they choose to work on. However, despite the clearly visible differences of quality, the level of completeness at the end of the three-day workshop was quite uniform among the groups: less than 20% of the groups have shown significant disadvantages compared to the aimed level. This is considered a progress compared to a similar workshop organized a few months before, and the difference can be associated to the presence of the Computational Concept Canvas tool. During the previous workshop, the absence of a strictly defined process (tool) resulted not particularly fruitful, wandering discussions in some of the groups. In the latter workshop, however, the defined format has helped many groups to identify autonomously their own difficulties, as these caused a visible blocking in the compilation of the canvas, so these students could turn to the tutors for clarifications. For the same reason, from the instructor's point of view, it was relatively easy to identify the groups to help, simply by observing their advance on the canvas. The specific questions that guide the work on the canvas also create a platform of discussion, which helps professors to switch rapidly between completely different topics, particularly important when the attention must be divided between numerous students, as this is an increasingly typical issue in the higher education of design.

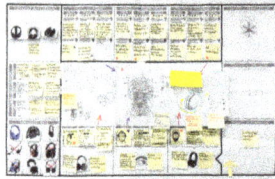

Students testing the first version of the canvas. Feedback was integrated to clarify some points and to slightly re-organize the modules, while maintaining most contents.

On the other hand, the workshop helped to surface some (precious) negative observations, part of which were integrated in the subsequent final version of the tool (presented in the previous chapter):

• difficulty of applying some of the analytical questions to some product categories;
• difficulty of reasoning in terms of 'variabilities' (rather than 'simple' improvements);
• sometimes misinterpreted suggestions, as limitations rather than stimuli;
• sometimes mechanical compilation of the fields, rather than critical discussion.

Therefore, on a general level we can assert that the canvas has fulfilled its main function of guiding the discussion in the desired direction, however we can also note the difficulty of the students to change their approach from developing single solutions (that respond specific problems) to wide solutions spaces (that respond variable requirements). Since the course started with an awareness of this difficulty, it was not surprising to observe it on the field. However, this also indicates that tackling with the problem of variable design would need a higher level of professional preparation of what third year bachelor students have, who are still in the process of solidifying their skills for a simpler, 'invariable' kind of design. More specifically, more experience would have been helpful with conceptual tools such as personas and user journey storyboarding, as well as with the technical tools such as para-metric modelling software. As far as the Canvas concerned, the previous critical feedback has stimulated its simplification and partial restructuring, which led to the final version of the canvas, already described in chapter 6-7.

Next steps

The Computational Concept Canvas tool provides a framework only for the first steps of a personalizable design project. After the ideation workshop, the Post Se-ries Design course continued with a more convention-al process of weekly meetings, during which students have elaborated firstly a 'static' 3D model simulating the personalizable product, then a parametric (per-sonalizable) model. In order to facilitate the discus-sion, students were asked to document each step of the development with a standard style of visualisation, that distinguishes with colors the variable parts (cyan) from the invariable parts (grey), and the interface where these two meet (magenta).

While the technology to use for the parametric model-ling can vary according to the business model suggested by the concept, in case of the Post Series Design course, all students used Grasshopper for Rhinoceros 3D. This simple but powerful approach to Computational Design allowed most students to create a variable geometry that is readily personalizable online using the platform ShapeDiver. This implies that with the currently avail-able software tools one product designer together with one web designer can easily design and market a per-sonalizable product for Digital Fabrication.

Of course, today the parametric approach is largely facilitated d by the evolution of software tools also beyond those used during the course. In chapter 3.6 we have examined them according to their level of ab-straction, which determines the effort needed for the acquisition and practice of the necessary knowledge. Their complexity ranges from simple parametric sol-id modelling (e.g. Solidworks, Fusion) to visual pro-gramming of generative geometries (e.g. Grasshop-per) until demanding but versatile direct code writing (e.g. Javascript). As far as the course concerned, wher-ever Grasshopper gave sub-optimal results, students

Development process of a student project (Eufonia), following the provided color scheme to distin-guish variable parts (cyan) from invariables (grey) and to show the interface between them (magenta).

Possible personalizations were illustrated with a gray-cyan-magenta color scheme. In this case, only cyan is used because the invariable technological core (essential oil diffuser) is entirely covered with a personalizable 3D printed plastic shell.

hypothesised which could be a more ideal path and which would be the requirements in that case. Finally, all projects were prototyped using Digital Fabrication tools, albeit not always the ones intended for the final production, due to budget limitations – and also because most projects included invariable functional components for serial manufacturing.

A brief selection of the student projects, also illustrated on the opposite page:

[1] *Blossom,* an essential oil diffuser that lets the user create a sort of artificial flower.[1]

[2] *Pixpie,* a 3D puzzle of personalizable shape, material and complexity.[2]

[3] *Eufonia,* a kettle that signals boiling water with a personalizable musical harmony.[3]

[4] *Mugnific,* a cup with personalizable proportions and parametric texture.[4]

[5] *Webbing,* a pair of headphones that adapts to the user's head shape.[5]

These were also exhibited at the MECSPE 2018 fair in Parma as part of Weerg's stand, to showcase the 3D printing technologies of this service bureau, as well as at the "Festival della Crescita 2018" in Rome and at the Roman edition of Maker Faire 2018. Some of the projects, are being developed further with the aim of commercial fruition, and some of the students also decided to dedicate their thesis projects to the topic of personalizable design. These instances can be considered as a positive feedback regarding the efficacy of the promoted "computational by design" approach.

[1] Giulia Chiacchiari, Sveva Guida
[2] Tullio Persiani, Sara Pignatone, Daniele Giovagnoli
[3] Gabriella Salvaggio, Isabella Ursano
[4] Sara Aiello, Mario Sbardella, Anna Maria Veltri
[5] Daniele Napolitano, Leonardo Simonetti, Simone Tiberia

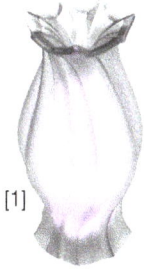

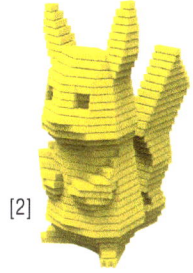

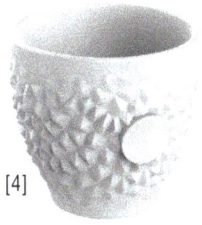

Twelve of the twenty projects designed during the Post Series Design course.
The numbered projects are described above, next to the respective numbering.

8.2 Design your Roman Holiday. A souvenir workshop.

This teaching experience helped to comprehend some of the difficulties in transmitting and conducting the design process focused on personalizability. The workshop was held before developing the Computational Concept Canvas, so it wasn't used yet; anyways, given the international participants and the limited timeframe, an open freeform interaction was preferable over following a strict format. In the beginning of 2017, we had the possibility to hold a 4-day international workshop for 24 students at Sapienza University of Rome. A similar workshop titled "Design your Roman Holiday" aims each year to improve the local tourist experience, considering the economic and social importance of this field in the city of Rome. Participants to this workshop are tourists themselves in some way: each year a different member of an inter-university collaboration is invited. The 2017 edition hosted 12 BSc students from the Oslo and Akershus University College of Applied Sciences, who worked with other 12 students of Sapienza University of Rome.[1]

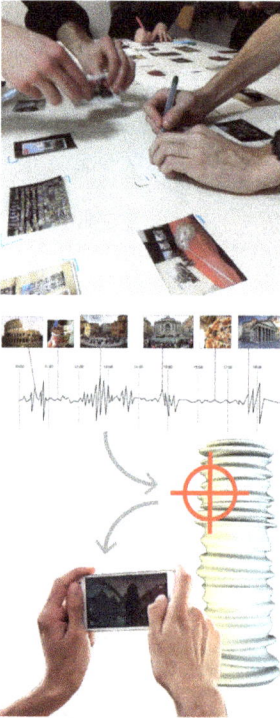

Analytical mapping of the collected souvenirs, in search for a better understanding of possible meanings. Below: the concept "Heartbeat"

The workshop theme was the conceptual design of personalizable souvenirs through Computational Design and Digital Fabrication, extending the usual workshop title to "Design your Roman Holiday *Memories*". The product typology of souvenirs is often despised due to the wide offer of cheap, poor quality mass products, stirring controversy for centuries. Today we can raise the question: considering all the available digital technologies, how would it be possible to make objects of memory more representative of the experiences of the user? Students were asked for contemporary and personalizable souvenirs imagined specifically for Computational Design and Digital Fabrication.

As preparation, the students (arranged in four-person groups, two Italians with two Norwegians) have examined the concept of "object of memory" by mapping and analysing their own personal souvenirs, thus helping to clarify their ideas regarding the possible values to offer to users. The mapping wasn't limited to any predefined format, except using post-it notes and printed photos of the souvenirs to be analyzed. Participants were asked to experiment freely with the arrangement of their souvenirs in the most adequate logical structure. In the aftermath we can note that, nonetheless the satisfying

[1] Beyond the author, workshop mentors were Prof. Einar Stoltenberg from Oslo, as well as Alex Coppola and Maria Zolotova from Sapienza University of Rome

results, mapping in a completely free format has slowed down the work, igniting not always fruitful discussions; this observation was fundamental for the later development of the Computational Concept Canvas, which can help significantly to optimise the time spent in the classroom and make advancement easier to track.

[1]

For the ideation after the analytical work, we have suggested two possible (opposite) approaches: starting from a product typology and finding a way to personalize it in a parametric way, or starting from a variable parameter of the tourist experience and finding object on which the variable can be applied. Foreseeing the possible product variations were rather challenging in the ideation phase, but at the end the groups managed to develop six fairly interesting concepts, with a level of detail obviously limited by available time. The following six concepts were elaborated, in order of the images on the right:

[2]

[1] *Heartbeat* transforms heartrate variability in a physical manifestation of the experience, similarly to the column of Trajan; this object, however, is interpretable with a smartphone application that connect the geometric features on the column to the specific experience by visualising photos corresponding to that moment.

[3]

[2] *Romap* records the GPS track of the tourist, transforming it in a personalized 3D map, thus recalling the journey and the visited monuments.

[3] *Mosaic* allows to construct a virtual cityscape, a mashup visualised through augmented reality based on the user's journey and the photos shot.

[4]

[4] *Alea* makes group decisions easier and more entertaining using a "guide" die, produced in advance to fit the interests.

[5] *Pastaroma* is a colander which can be morphed to different shapes and patterns, derived from characteristic visual clues of the city, chosen from a library or uploaded by the user.

[5]

[6] *Sampietrini* invites the user to detach a fragment from a typical Roman cobblestone, at a specialised shop. This humble material becomes a precious stone when integrated in a digitally personalizable jewel.

[6]

The six concepts covered a wide range of approaches, both regarding the personalization principle and the typology of the result:

- from utilitarian objects to decorative and playful ones with a narrative;
- through a personalization experience ranging from automatic-computational to creative-proactive;
- produced in different moments: before, during or after the visit;
- in established typologies or completely new ones.

The workshop led to some important observations and challenges:

- comprehending the exact breadth of technological possibilities;
- choosing of starting point for the ideation;
- choosing the right incentives for the users;
- foreseeing the range of forms that might result from the possible user inputs;
- discussing the flexible project, more complicated than reviewing 'static' deisgn.

These observations were fundamental for elaborating a more articulated workflow and the Computational Concept Canvas. The workshop raised the necessity of a tool that could guide the flow of discussion and stimulate students to consider a wide variety of factors that might go otherwise unnoticed, if following the usual mindset of design for serial production. To sum up, in this section we have seen how a product typology that might be considered cheap and banal could offer the possibility to hypothesise a wide range of interesting products that would be impossible without Digital Fabrication and Computational Design.

8.3 Mapping the progress

The renewed design approach proposed by this book is based on the observation that personalizable products existing on the market have already demonstrated that Computational Design enables new ways of sensible response to divergent desires. As detailed in chapter 4, these case studies could be arranged according to six types of variabilities divided in two groups, distinguishing between personalization for primarily mechanical aspects and primarily cognitive aspects. These variabilities respond to different user motivations, leading to different personalization principles to be followed by the designers. Through didactic activities and personal practice, the author has contributed to the development of over 30 personalizable projects, all of which can be evaluated according to the system of six variabilities. As intended, these projects covered all the identified personalization principles, demonstrating that a conscious effort of valorising Computational Design and Digital Fabrication can lead to new opportunities in many product typologies across the material culture. The scheme on the next page illustrates how a selection of these projects expand the world of personalizable design, relating them also to the previously described case studies; as with these, secondary motivations for each case study are illustrated on a radar diagram.

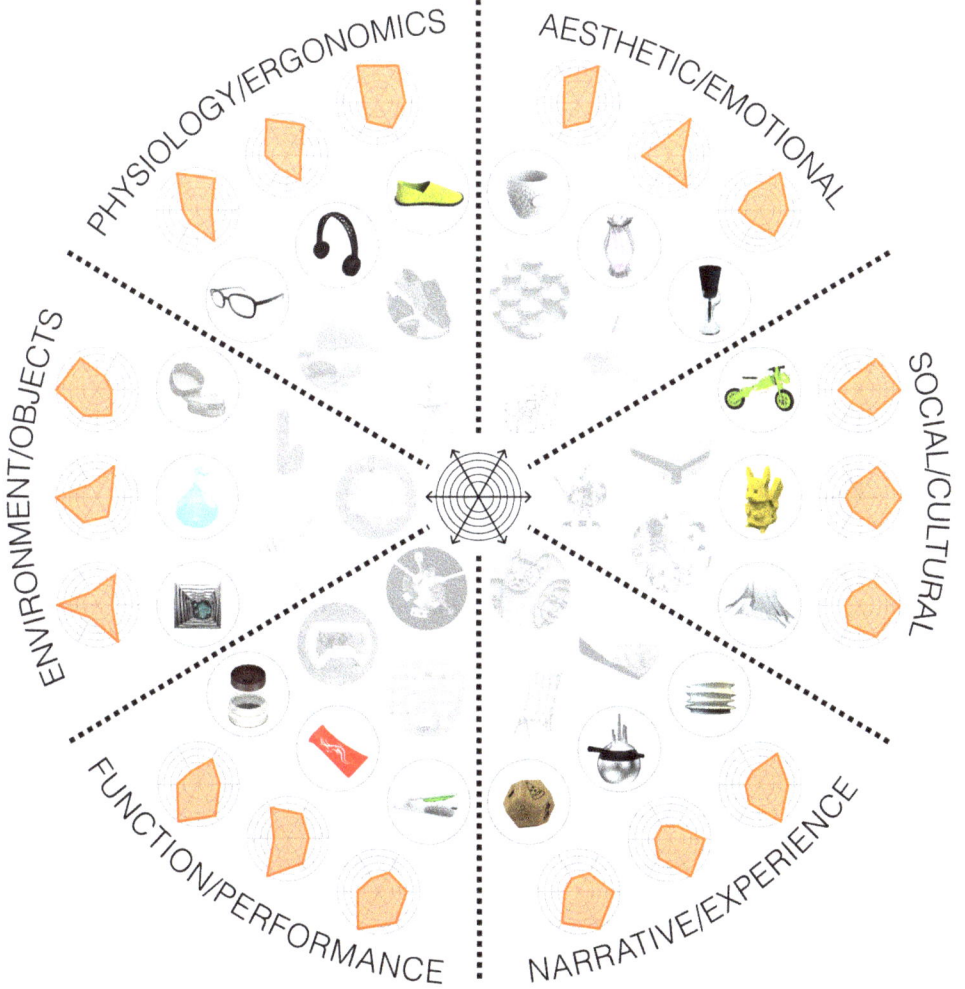

personalization
for dominantly
MECHANICAL
aspects

personalization
for dominantly
COGNITIVE
aspects

PHYSIOLOGY/ERGONOMICS

AESTHETIC/EMOTIONAL

ENVIRONMENT/OBJECTS

SOCIAL/CULTURAL

FUNCTION/PERFORMANCE

NARRATIVE/EXPERIENCE

CONCLUSIONS

Overview

This book started with the observation that, despite the diffusion of new digital technologies in manufacturing, the promise of a paradigm shift between design, production and consumption has not yet changed much the everyday material culture for most people. To facilitate the proliferation of digital dynamics also in shaping physical objects of use, we have identified personalization as a key concept. Considering this vision, the Design profession could help valorising Digital Fabrication and Computational Design, of which the practical use is still much behind compared to the advanced examples of academic and artistic research.

This, however, requires a twofold effort from the discipline: on one hand it's necessary to recognise that the creative capabilities in this field are strongly determined by the knowledge of technical tools, not only of Digital Fabrication, but also of Computational Design (or parametric/generative modelling), which can be practiced at different levels of difficulty, thus implying a variety of corresponding business models. On the other hand, it's necessary to recognise the asymmetry between the advanced technological tools and the lacking conceptual tools. The book attempts to fill this gap, offering a design approach, to practice with a new tool, which can be useful for developing personalizable products across many product categories, thus creating new entrepreneurial opportunities, relying on the increasingly mainstream industry 4.0 technologies. Hence, maybe the most relevant use of the proposed tool is contributing to the (recently planned) education of a new generation of professionals who will be capable of valorising this digital evolution of the contemporary industry.

While trusting the utility of the described design approach and tool, the encountered difficulties are worth noting. So, apart from the key lessons, also some of the emerging issues are discussed in the next section, hoping that this might be useful for directing future research and the practical implementation of personalizable design in enterprises, as well as in higher education.

Takeaways and issues

A design method and tool for the concept development focused on Computational Design and Digital Fabrication: The most important takeaway of this book is the Computational Concept Canvas tool, which helps to valorise user divergence as a design material leading to wide solutions spaces. To enable practicing the approach in a variety of contexts also beyond the classroom, the Computational Concept Canvas toolkit is distributed free with a Creative Commons license, including a synthetic guideline and a variety of canvas formats, all with the same structure but with different dimensions to allow working at different levels of detail. The canvas was developed through various didactic activities of the author, which first highlighted the necessity of a consciously structured workflow, a need addressed later through the canvas which was tested and evolved during other teaching activities. While the canvas facilitates the work, there are some issues without any clear solution in sight; these might be inherent difficulties of designing for personalizability:

- difficulty to apply certain types of variability on certain product categories;
- difficulty of reasoning in terms of variabilities, rather than simple improvements;
- tendency of students to fill in the canvas fields mechanically, rather than critically;
- difficulty to understand conceptual possibilities without a deep practical knowledge in Computational Design technologies.

Another limitation derives from the fact that the Canvas is based on the idea of comprehending personalization principles in projects done by others, then systemically evaluating the applicability of these principles to existing product typologies. This logic tends to promote incremental innovation rather than radical innovation. Therefore, it's clear that further work should be done in the field, especially because in the end only commercially successful products could prove whether the tool can contribute to the diffusion of personalizable design. But even in a didactic environment, the canvas can help to build a series of projects which, if well publicised, might stimulate companies to start thinking in 'on-demand design'.

Case studies that highlight the possible user motivations for using Computational Design: The collection and analysis of case studies (chapter 4) have helped to identify a useful system of six types of product variabilities, responding to either mechanical or cognitive user divergences. This system is the basis of the analytical work on the Canvas; the product sheets demonstrate practical manifestations of each kind of variability, so these are useful illustration for teaching personalizable design, and they could be useful also to persuade client firms. Of course, these examples are neither exhaustive nor representative of the market: while three products were included for each kind of variability, some of these today have far more examples than others. However, this quantitative distortion might help discovering less common user divergences, thus going beyond the most obvious ideas and arriving to more 'original' ones.

Tools and workflows for the technical implementation of the concepts coming from the Canvas: Chapter 3.6 has outlined some possible tools for practicing personalizable, computational product design, recognising that these software can be organized in three groups according to the level of abstraction required from the designer, levels which determine also the required effort for learning and practicing these tools – as experienced by the author personally, through various projects. On the other hand, higher levels of abstraction enable more interesting morphologies and a wider diffusion of the project through web applications. Respectively varies also the available range of possible business models: from the digital artisan's (work)shop to entirely automatized web-based projects which outsource also the manufacturing to online services. The web-based Computational Design solutions are still in their infancy; the cited tools will hopefully evolve and there might be new ones coming. Notably, there are some embryonal experiments for native Grasshopper-style visual programming on the web, which could enable far more fluid modelling and interactions than current solutions; designers interested in Computational Design should be scanning regularly the evolution of the available technical tools. These were not central to this book, but aiming for wider diffusion, a publication would be useful to offer a wider and more detailed collection of computational tools with a product design perspective, in order to help crucial strategic choices of enterprises as well as designers wishing to learn new tools.

Speaking of strategic choices, let's remember that chapter 6.6 has connected schematically the fields of the Canvas with the renewed process of design-production-distribution, highlighting not only possible design tools, but also possible relations with the manufacturing resources and possible channels of personalization and distribution.

Professional evolution

The book has developed the hypotheses that designing personalizable products could become a solid practice with consistent results, but this would need both 'well-structured' digital drawings and a concept design approach that is more sensitive to divergent user needs. By elaborating a method and a tool, the book aimed to improve the design process to consistently widen the range of products that valorise Digital Fabrication through Computational Design. However, in order to consolidate the practice, further steps will be necessary, not only in the professional world, but also in the world of research, to verify more widely the new knowledge, especially in an entrepreneurial context. While the proposed method is based on a set of variabilities extracted from case studies, future research could extend or refine this set of key characteristics, or it could develop entirely new ways of discovering meanings for personalization, or it could promote the exploration of entirely new "computational" qualities in product design.

This evolution will likely promote a different nature of the design profession, by increasing its sensibility towards divergences between users, and by increasing its virtuosity in handling complex geometries accordingly. Whether and which new skills can be integrated into the core of the design profession is an open question. Today, emerging technologies allow a single (well-trained) designer to rapidly switch between many tasks that would have required separate professionals twenty years ago. Similarly, Digital Fabrication and Computational Design can be transformative – not only as productivity tools, but also as promoters of a different 'nature' of design.

The necessary new technical and conceptual skills might require a further branching of the discipline, which would be a natural and welcome sign of maturation.

The book stemmed from the belief that the (product) designer's use of Computational Design should focus on celebrating the wide variety of values appreciated by different users – hence the title Computational *by* Design. Computational tools can act as design partners, which can continuously re-shape a product's design, potentially even in distant places or times, so even physical products can become a question of software, which can be developed gradually, maintaining the product eternally in a beta testing phase. Consequently changes the nature of participation, which can integrate continuously the people's changing desires through the design interfaces used for personalization. On the long term, a Computational *by* Design attitude might enable a more 'on-demand' material culture, promoting a more active role of the user in shaping it both functionally and semantically, thus establishing a deeper connection between people and their objects through new kinds of personal narratives.

REFERENCES

Aish, R. and Woodbury, R. (2005). Multi-level Interaction in Parametric Design. In A. Butz, B. Fisher, A. Krüger, P. Olivier (edited by), *Smart Graphics,* pp. 924-924. Berlin: Springer

Amiri, F. (2011). Programming as Design: The Role of Programming in Interactive Media Curriculum in Art and Design. *International Journal of Art & Design Education,* 30, 2011, 200-210.

Anderson, C. (2006). *The Long Tail: Why the Future of Business Is Selling Less of More.* New York: Hyperion.

Anderson, C. (2012). *Makers: The New Industrial Revolution.* Danvers: Crown Publishing Group.

Andreessen, M. (2011). Why Software Is Eating the World. In *The Wall Street Journal,* August 20, 2011 http://online.wsj.com/article/SB10001424053111903 480904576512250915629460.html This

Ängeslevä, J., Nicenboim, I., Wunderling, J., Lindlbauer, D., (2016). Beyond Prototyping. In C. Gengnagel, E. Nagy, R. Stark (eds.), Rethinking Prototyping—New Hybrid Concepts for Prototyping. Switzerland: Springer International Publishing.

Armstrong, A., Hagel, J. (1999). The Real Value of On-Line Communities. In D. Tapscott (edited by), *Creating Value in the Network Economy.* pp. 173-185. Boston, MA: Harvard Business School Publishing.

Baudrillard, J. (1968). *Le système des objects.* Paris: éditions Gallimard. English translation by James Benedict. *The System of Objects.* London: Verso, 1996/2002.

Bjögvinsson, E., Ehn, P. & Hillgren, P. (2012). Design Things And Design Thinking: Contemporary Participatory Design Challenge. *Design Issues* 28, 3 (Summer 2012), 101-116. DOI: http://dx.doi.org/10.1162/DESI_a_00165

Bowyer, A. (2007). *The Self-replicating Rapid Prototyper — Manufacturing for the Masses,* Invited Keynote Address, Proc. 8th National Conference on Rapid Design, Prototyping & Manufacturing, Centre for Rapid Design and Manufacture, High Wycombe, June 2007. Rapid Prototyping and Manufacturing Association.

Branzi, A. e Hara, K. (2016). *Neo Preistoria: 100 Verbi.* Lars Muller Publishers.

Brereton, M., Buur, J. (2008). New Challenges for Design Participation in the Era of Ubiquitous Computing. *CoDesign* 4, 2 (2008): 112.

Brown, T. (2009). *Change by Design: How Design Thinking Transforms Organizations and Inspires Innovation.* New York: Harper Collins.

Brynjolfsson, E., McAfee, A. (2014). *The Second Machine Age: Work, Progress, and Prosperity in a Time of Brilliant Technologies.* New York: Norton & Company.

Burry, M. (2013). *Scripting Cultures: Architectural Design and Programming.* John Wiley & Sons

Carpo, M. (2015). *The Alphabet and the Algorithm.* MIT Press, Cambridge.

Chapman, J. (2005). *Emotionally Durable Design. Objects, Experiences and Empathy.* London: Eartchscan.

Clune, J., Lipson, H. (2011). Evolving three-dimensional objects with a generative encoding inspired by developmental biology. In T. Lenaerts, M. Giacobini, H. Bersini, P. Bourgine, M. Dorigo, R. Doursat (edited by), *Proceedings of the European Conference on Artificial Life.* pp. 141-148. Cambridge, MA: MIT Press.

Cross, N. (2007). From a design science to a design discipline: Understanding designerly ways of knowing and thinking. In R. Michel (edited by) *Design Research Now*, 41-54. Basel: Birkhäuser.

Cruickshank, L. (2014). *Open design and innovation.* London: Routledge.

Davis, D. (2013). *A History of Parametric.* Retrieved from http://www.danieldavis.com/a-history-of-parametric/

Davis, S. M. (1987). *Future perfect.* Boston: Addison-Wesley.

Davis, S. M. (2007). *Interview at MCPC 2007.* Retrieved from http://www.configurator-database.com/scientific/stan-davis-future-mass-customization

De Mul, J. (2011). Redesigning design. In B. Abel (edited by), *Open design now.* Amsterdam: BIS.

Di Lucchio, L. (2014). Design on-demand. Evoluzioni possibili tra design, produzione e consumo. In T. Paris (edited by), *Lectures#2*, pp. 62-77. Rome: Rdesignpress.

DiSalvo, C., Maki, J., Martin, N. (2007). Mapmover: A Case Study of Design-Oriented Research into Collective Expression and Constructed Publics. In R. Grinter, T. Rodden, P. Aoki, E. Cutrell, R. Jeffries, G. Olsons (edited by), *Proceedings of the SIGCHI Conference on Human Factors in Computing Systems*, pp. 1249-52. New York: ACM.

Fischer, G. & Ostwald, J. (2002). Seeding, evolutionary growth, and reseeding: Enriching participatory design with informed participation. *Proceedings of PDC 2002*, pp. 135-143. Palo Alto, CA: CPSR.

Fischer, G. (2009). End-User Development and Meta-design: Foundations for Cultures of Participation. In V. Pipek et al. (edited by), *IS-EUD 2009, LNCS 5435*, pp. 3–14, 2009. Berlin: Springer-Verlag.

Fischer, G., Giaccardi, E. (2006). Meta-Design: A Framework for the Future of End User Development. In: Lieberman, H., Paternò, F., Wulf, V. (edited by), *End User Development*, pp. 427–457. Dordrecht: Kluwer Academic Publishers.

Foster, F. (2016). The Selfish Ledger. [video for Google X]. Retrieved 23 November, 2018, from https://www.theverge.com/2018/5/17/17344250/google-x-selfish-ledger-video-data-privacy

Friedman, K. (2008). Research into, by and for design. *Journal of Visual Art Practice*, 7(2), 153-160.

Garbee, E. (2016). *This Is Not the Fourth Industrial Revolution*. Retrieved from http://www.slate.com/articles/technology/future_tense/2016/01/the_world_economic_forum_is_wrong_this_isn_t_the_fourth_industrial_revolution.html

Gershenfeld, N. (2005). *Fab: The Coming Revolution on Your Desktop--from Personal Computers to Personal Fabrication*. New York: Basic Books.

Gershenfeld, N. (2012). How to Make Almost Anything. *Foreign Affairs*, November/December 2012, pp. 43-57

Gilmore, J. H. & Pine, J. B. (2007). *Authenticity: contending with the new consumer sensibility*. Boston: Harvard Business Review Press.

Granelli, A. (2010). *Artigiani del digitale. Come creare valore con le nuove tecnologie*. Roma: Luca Sossella editore.

Hess, J., Pipek, V. (2012). Community-Driven Development: Approaching Participatory Design in the Online World. *Design Issues*, 28, 3 (Summer 2012), pp. 62-76. doi: http://dx.doi.org/10.1162/DESI_a_00162

Holman, W. (2015). Makerspace: Towards a New Civic Infrastructure. *Places Journal*, November 2015. Retrieved from https://doi.org/10.22269/151130

IDEO (2015). *The Field Guide to Human-Centered Design*. Retrieved from http://www.designkit.org

Iordanova, I. (2007). Teaching Digital Design Exploration: Form Follows. *International Journal of Architectural Computing*, 5, 2007, 685-702.

Jonas, W. (2007). From a design science to a design discipline: Understanding designerly ways of knowing and thinking. In R. Michel (edited by) *Design Research Now*, 41-54. Basel: Birkhäuser.

Jones, J. C. (1970). *Design Methods: seeds of human futures*. London: John Wiley & Sons.

Jones, J. C., Thornley, D. (edited by) (1962). *The Conference on Design Methods: papers presented at the conference on systematic and intuitive methods in engineering, industrial design, architecture and communications.* London: Pergamon Press.

Kay, A. (1984). Computer Software. *Scientific American*, Volume 251, n.3

Keinonen, T., Takala R. (2006). *Product concept design: a review of the conceptual design of products in industry.* London: Springer-Verlag.

Kelley, T. (2013). *Creative Confidence: Unleashing the Creative Potential Within Us All.* New York: Harper Collins.

Koen, P., Ajamian, G., Burkart, R., Clamen, A., Davidson, J., D'Amore, R., Elkins, C., Herald, K., Incorvia, M., Johnson, A., Karol, R., Seibert, R., Slavejkov, A., Wagner K. (2001). Providing clarity and a common language to the 'fuzzy front end'. *Research Technology Management*, 44(2):46-55

Krippendorff, K. (2005). *The Semantic Turn: A New Foundation for Design.* UK: Taylor & Francis

Kuma, V. (2012). *101 Design Methods: A Structured Approach for Driving Innovation in Your Organization.* Hoboken: John Wiley & Sons.

Lee, J. H., Gu, N., Williams, A. P. (2013). Exploring design strategy in Parametric Design to Support Creativity. In: R. Stouffs, P. H. T. Janssen, S. Roudavski, B. Tunçer (edited by), *Open Systems: CAADRIA 2013*, pp. 489-498. Singapore

Lee, J., Gu, N., Williams, A. P. (2014). Parametric design strategies for the generation of creative designs. *International Journal of Architectural Computing*, 12(3), 263-282. doi:10.1260/1478-0771.12.3.263

Levi-Strauss, C. (1962). *La pensee sauvage.* Paris: Plon.

Lipson, H., Kurman, M. (2013). *Fabricated: The New World of 3D Printing.* Indianapolis: John Wiley & Sons.

Liu,Y. T., Lim, C. K. (2006). New tectonics: a preliminary framework involving classic and digital thinking. *Design Studies*, 27, 2006, 267-307.

Llach, D. C. (2013). Algorithmic tectonics: How Cold War Era Research Shaped Our Imagination of Design. In B. Peters, X. De Kestelier (edited by), *Architectural Design Special Issue: Computation Works: The Building of Algorithmic Thought*, p 16-21. Indianapolis: John Wiley & Sons.

Lynn, G. (1993). *Folding in Architecture.* Academy Editions

Maeda, J. (2001). *Design by Numbers.* Boston: MIT Press.

Maeda, J., Xu, J, Gilboa, A., Kabba, F, Sayarath, J. (2017). Design in Tech Report 2017. Retrieved 23 November, 2018, from https://designintech.report/wp-content/uploads/2017/03/dit-2017-1-0-7-compressed.pdf

Maldonado, T. (1992). *Reale e virtuale*. Milano: Giangiacomo Feltrinelli Editore.

Manovich, L. (2013). *Software takes command: extending the language of new media*. New York: Bloomsbury Academic.

Manzini, E. (2015). *Design, When Everybody Designs*. Cambridge, MA: MIT Press.

Martin, B., Hanington, B. (2012). *Universal Methods of Design*. Beverly: Rockport Publishers.

McCullough, M. (1996). *Abstracting Craft: The Practiced Digital Hand*. Cambridge, MA: MIT Press.

Micelli, S. (2011). *Futuro artigiano*. Venezia: Marsilio Editori.

Murray, R., Caulier-Grice, J., Mulgan, G. (2010). *The Open Book Of Social Innovation*. 1st ed. UK: NESTA.

Osterwalder, A., Pigneur, Y. (2010). *Business Model Generation: A Handbook for Visionaries, Game Changers, and Challengers*. Wiley.

Osterwalder, A., Pigneur, Y., Bernarda, G., Smith, A., Papadakos, T. (2014). *Value Proposition Design: How to Create Products and Services Customers Want*, John Wiley & Sons.

Oxman, N. (2010). *Material-based Design Computation*. Ph.D. thesis, MIT.

Pine, J. B. & Gilmore, J. H. (1999). *The experience economy*. Boston: Harvard Business School Press.

Pine, J. B. (1992). *Mass Customization: The New Frontier in Business Competition*. Boston: Harvard Business School Press.

Pine, J. B., Korn, K. C. (2011). *Infinite Possibility. Creating Customer Value on the Digital Frontier*. San Francisco: Berrett-Koehler.

Pye, D. W. (1968). *The Nature and Art of Workmanship*. Cambridge University Press

Riesman, D., Denny, R., Glazer, N. (1950). The Lonely Crowd: A Study of the Changing American Character. (New Haven: Yale University Press/London: Geoffrey Cumberlege, Oxford University Press, 1950), p. 46.

Salvador, F., de Holan, P. M., Piller F. (2009). Cracking the Code of Mass Customization. *MIT Sloan Management Review*, 50(3), 2009, pp. 70–79.

Scheibehenne, B., Greifeneder, R., Todd, P. M. (2010). Can There Ever be Too Many Options? A Meta-Analytic Review of Choice Overload. *Journal of Consumer Research*. 37: 409–425. doi:10.1086/651235

Schumacher, P. (2016). *Parametricism 2.0: Rethinking Architecture's Agenda for the 21st Century*. Indianapolis: John Wiley & Sons.

Schwab, K. (2017). *The Fourth Industrial Revolution*. US: Crown.

Schwartz, B. (2004). *The Paradox of Choice - Why More Is Less*. New York: Harper Perennial.

Sennett, R. (2008). *The Craftsman*. New Haven: Yale University Press.

Shiner, L. (2007). The fate of craft. In S. Alfoldy (edited by), *NeoCraft: Modernity and the Crafts*, pp. 33-46. Halifax: NSCAD Press.

Singh P. J., Gurumurthy, A. (2013). Establishing Public-ness in the Network: New Moorings for Development - A Critique of the Concepts of Openness and Open Development. In M. L. Smith, K. M. A. Reilly (edited by), *Open Development: Networked Innovations in International Development*, Cambridge, MA: MIT Press.

Stappers, P. E., Giaccardi, E. (2017). Research through Design. In AA. VV. *The Encyclopedia of Human-Computer Interaction, 2nd Ed.*, https://www.interac-tion-design.org/literature/book/the-encyclopedia-of-human-computer-interac-tion-2nd-ed/research-through-design

Sterling, B. (2005). *Shaping Things*. Cambridge: MIT Press.

Sutherland, I. (1975). Structure in Drawing and the Hidden-Surface Problem. In N. Negroponte (edited by), *Reflections on Computer Aids to Design and Architecture*, pp. 73-77. New York: Petrocelli/Charter.

Tassi, R. (2008). *Design della comunicazione e design dei servizi. Il progetto della comunicazione per l'implementazione*. Laurea Magistrale, Politecnico di Milano.

Tedeschi, A., Wirz, F., Andreani, S. (2014). *AAD, Algorithms-aided design*. Brienza: Le Penseur.

Toffler, A. (1980). *The Third Wave*. New York: Morrow.

Visocky O 'Grady, J., Visocky O'Grady, K. (2006). *A designer's research manual: succeed in design by knowing your client and what they really need*. Gloucester: Rockport Publishers.

Yenicioglu, B, Suerdem, A. (2015). Participatory New Product Development - A Framework for Deliberately Collaborative and Continuous Innovation Design. *Procedia - Social and Behavioral Sciences* 195 (2015) pp. 1443 – 1452

Yoon, HS., Lee, JY., Kim, HS., Shin, YJ., Chu, WS., Ahn SH. (2014). A comparison of energy consumption in bulk forming, subtractive, and additive processes: Review and case study.
International Journal of Precision Engineering and Manufacturing 1: 261. https://doi.org/10.1007/s40684-014-0033-0

INDEX

www.ingramcontent.com/pod-product-compliance
Lightning Source LLC
Chambersburg PA
CBHW050645190326
41458CB00008B/2435